THE
LONG
and the
SHORT
OF IT

THE
LONG
and the
SHORT
OF IT

ANDY NORTH
with **Burton Rocks**

THOMAS DUNNE BOOKS   ST. MARTIN'S PRESS   NEW YORK

THOMAS DUNNE BOOKS.
An imprint of St. Martin's Press.

www.stmartins.com

Library of Congress Cataloging-in-Publication Data

North, Andy.
 The long and short of it / Andy North with Burton Rocks.—1st ed.
  p. cm.
 ISBN 0-312-28797-6
 1. Golf. I. Rocks, Burton. II. Title.

GV962.3 .N67   2002
796.352—dc21

2001048873

First Edition: May 2002

10 9 8 7 6 5 4 3 2 1

This book is dedicated to the three special women in my life:
Nichole and Andrea, my daughters, who prove daily,
great children don't come cheap;

and Susan, my best friend, my lover, my goddess, my wife.

—ANDY

To Mom and Dad, Marlene and Dr. Lawrence Rocks,
the greatest parents on earth, who make being
a young author so enjoyable.

Mom, thanks for your loving support and guidance
throughout my childhood.

Dad, for "the three things," for being an acclaimed author role
model, and for "Willie and Gloria," your greatest gift to me.

I thank God every day for Mom and Dad.

—BURTON

Contents

CONTENTS

Foreword

It is one of the most select clubs in all of golf—those who have won more than one U.S. Open. Jack Nicklaus, of course, heads the list with four victories. It's the same number for Ben Hogan, Bobby Jones, and Willie Anderson, who turned the trick at the turn of the last century.

Hale Irwin won three, and then there's the group of two that includes Lee Trevino, Gene Sarazen, Walter Hagen, Billy Casper, Curtis Strange, Ernie Els, and Andy North.

Andy North? How is it possible that someone who has won three times on tour did it twice at the grueling U.S. Open?

Andy North? It's possible that of all eighteen men who have won multiple U.S. Opens, certainly in the modern era, he was the least well known when he registered his second U.S. Open win.

Andy North? There is more remembered about T. C. Chen, the man who lost the lead in 1985 with his infamous "two chip," than there is about North in his victory.

So why a book about Andy North? I would have said the same thing until I first worked with him on a U.S. Open Preview Show for ESPN in 1994. It didn't take long for me to realize that he was one of the most engaging, observant, introspective, and downright funny individuals I had ever worked with; in fact, I start looking forward to working each U.S. Open months before June, and the opportunity to work alongside and spend maybe fourteen hours a day with Andy for the better part of a week is a big reason why.

Included inside is, obviously, the 1978 and 1985 U.S. Opens, both of which North won by just one stroke. At Cherry Hills, he won as a front-runner, leading by two at the halfway mark over three others, including Jack Nicklaus. After fifty-four holes, his lead was just one over another living legend, Gary Player, whom he was paired with on the final day.

At Oakland Hills, North did it coming from behind, trailing Chen by as many as four strokes early Sunday until the Taiwanese player suffered his self-inflicted disaster on the front nine. He ended up beating three players by just that one stroke in 1985, and two by that thin margin in his first win in 1978, which meant that every swing was critical. You'll relive all those moments through North's eyes and more.

But make no mistake, the point of this text is not to be a historical record of the 1978 and 1985 U.S. Opens. If golf mimics life, then Andy North hits every type of shot with every club in the bag. His observations, lessons, and stories come from the fairways, the rough, and the bunkers.

Golf demands that you think, which you'll do here. It demands that you laugh, which you'll certainly do here. It can sometimes make you cry, but one hopes that will be limited here.

One thing's for sure. To win two U.S. Opens takes a very special talent. After reading what follows, you'll agree that Andy North has that as a storyteller as well as a golfer. You'll also wonder why you overlooked him all these years.

—CHRIS BERMAN

Acknowledgments

First, and foremost, we want to thank Chris Berman for graciously writing a terrific foreword to this book and for his guidance and insight. We wish to thank literary agent Tony Seidl for always believing in this project and for getting it into the hands of St. Martin's Press, and particularly Pete Wolverton.

A heartfelt thanks to Pete Wolverton, associate publisher of Thomas Dunne Books, for his guidance, understanding, and exceptional insight. We couldn't have done it without you, Pete. Thanks to Carolyn Dunkley at Thomas Dunne Books for her patience and friendly help throughout this process. Thanks to Joseph Rinaldi at St. Martin's Press for terrific marketing, and to the rest of his staff for their tireless promotion of this book, golf caps included.

Thanks to Soupy Sales, Mickey Freeman, Freddie Roman, Jean-Pierre Trebot, Michael Caputo, Mark Shatsky, Jack L. Green, and our pal Gianfranco Capitelli at the New York Friars Club for graciously hosting our photo shoot for the inside flap of this book.

Thanks to photographer Bob Hall for a job well done on the photograph of us.

Thanks to all the folks at ESPN for their support of this project and to the folks at CNBC as well for their continued partnership with the SENIOR PGA TOUR. Thanks to the USGA and the PGA TOUR, as well as to the SENIOR PGA TOUR for their support.

Thanks to friends and family who encouraged us along the way and to the many golf fans all over the world for supporting golf.

Andy North and Burton Rocks

Introduction

All I needed to do was make a three-foot putt to win the U.S. Open. I had just hit out of the sand, where my major concern was to keep the ball below the hole. I had accomplished that, and now, with the wind howling, I stood over my putt, ready to become the champion. The wind didn't make it easy for me. I backed away three times before I calmly stroked the ball into the hole. I was now, and forever would be, a U.S. Open champion.

When preparing for the U.S. Open a player usually tries to be in the best mental and physical condition possible. I had been playing well, with a second place finish in Charlotte two weeks before the Open. I then took the week off to prepare myself mentally to be on that fine edge that either takes you to victory or leaves you in the depths of despair at the Open. My physical preparation was a different matter. Food poisoning was not on my list of ways to prepare for the Open. But, food poisoning it was. I thought all my preparation was going down the drain.

Just when life is at its bleakest, you sometimes find a shining light. When the doctor told me as a child I had a bone disease and had to quit playing sports I thought that my life was over. At twelve, what else was there to do? After pleading with the doctor to let me do something, he decided playing golf, using a cart, wouldn't hurt me. So I spent every waking hour that summer on the golf course. It gave me not only a newfound sense of purpose, it gave me the basis for a great life. I have had great success and made friendships that I treasure deeply. The places I've visited and my life experiences are priceless. I have been able to provide a wonderful, fulfilling life for me and my family that might never have happened if my twelfth summer had been spent on the baseball field.

Little did I know in my fiftieth year I would meet another shining light. A law school graduate named Burton Rocks called me and said he wanted to write a book. About me! I told him I didn't want to do a book and thought that it would end there. Well, Burton wanted to do a book, and he kept calling me and bugging me to talk with him. I finally gave in and said I would meet him. It became obvious to me that it would be easier to say yes to Burton and do the book than to have him keep bugging me. I hope that you all agree with Burton and enjoy reading what we have to say.

—ANDY NORTH

Part One

My Story

Behind every professional golfer is a story of perseverance and courage.

1. Not Your Average Golfing Story

Golf, for me, was not a sport of first choice, but rather one that was adaptable to my physical condition. The love of the game that is often referred to came, for me, right after I was diagnosed with a rare bone disease.

My father, Dr. Stewart North, and my mother, Mary, gave me the fundamental values that both my sister Pam, now an M.D., and I would carry with us and would enable us to build exciting futures for ourselves in our twenties. My family's firm foundation, even when fame and fortune came my way through golf, kept me grounded at all times. My father and mother were both educators. My dad holds a Ph.D. and taught for years at the University of Wisconsin, in their graduate department, and my mother taught high school home economics. Mom and Dad gave me the love, encouragement, spirituality, and support necessary for me to venture out on my own in my early twenties and try my hand at professional golf.

I was a kid who grew up in a family in which involvement in sports was encouraged by both my parents. My father was my coach, and I was always partaking in some athletic event. Whether it was running track in the spring, playing football in the fall, or playing baseball in the summer, Dad and I could always be found together as a team. I loved sports and loved him because he made them enjoyable for me. My dad was my mentor and pal. Life at age ten seemed perfect.

I can't pinpoint the specific date or week that my life became drastically changed, but I remember the intense pain in my left knee. To say I began having trouble with my knee is to put it mildly. I had this pronounced limp, which my dad noticed while I was playing basketball, that just rapidly worsened with time. It reached a critical stage where we had to consult our physician, who in turn performed a series of rather involved tests on my knee. The result of two weeks of these tests: discovery of a rare bone disease.

The disease was called *osteo chrondritis disicance*. In laymen's terms it meant that there was a small portion of bone in the joint of my left knee that was degenerating very quickly. This was due to a lack of proper blood supply to that area. No one knew why this condition struck me. We did know that the immediate response had to be a sudden stoppage of all physical activity that placed any extra stress on my knee.

I was only twelve years old at the time, and the diagnosis was devastating. Instead of playing ball, I would be hobbling around on crutches for the next few years of my life. But often, life doesn't give people a choice. I had no choice. It was either the crutches or just stay at home and do nothing.

I didn't have many medical options open to me, either. One possible decision my physician presented was to undergo surgery and have the bone in my left knee that was degenerating cut out. At that time this type of operation was viewed as a radical option. Surgery didn't make much sense, either, because if anything went wrong the side effects were just too grave. The other option presented to us was for me to just accept my condition and use crutches on a permanent basis. This was exactly what I chose—and for good reason. I spent all of seventh and eighth grade using those crutches, and to say that it was devastating me is an understatement. It seemed as if the love of sports I had had up until that point was being washed away with this disease.

My weekends were suddenly reduced to hobbling over to the refrigerator and peering inside to see what was for lunch.

While I was hobbling around on crutches, the idea of being an athlete seemed almost ludicrous. I even bought a book that listed all of the possible sports, the equivalent of a world sports almanac. I went through the book with my doctor one sport at a time. Each time I asked him if "this" was a possible sport for me, he answered with a resounding no. It was demoralizing. Sport after sport, the answer was the same. That day in his office seemed like an eternity. "Doc, can I play this?" "No," he would reply. Then I came upon the game of golf, however, and something surprising happened. He kind of scratched his head and after a rather long pause he said that I could play golf. He said it was the one sport that would not stress my knee. However, there was one condition, and a big one. I could play golf as long as I used a cart, because golf required an inordinate amount of walking. The only way to overcome the constant walking was to use a cart. That way I could hit my shot then hop in my cart and take off down the fairway towards the next shot. The cart was the answer! However, my young age was a tremendous obstacle to overcome when it came to the use of carts. The clubs didn't even let healthy thirteen-year-olds ride golf carts on a golf course. It was just something that clubs felt went against golf protocol.

Before that day in the doctor's office I had played a few rounds of golf with my dad, who himself had been a good golfer as a young adult. He had left the game for a while but decided he wanted to play golf again. So we were in the process of joining a club in Madison, Wisconsin, when I was diagnosed with this bone disease. I started taking lessons from the club pro, Lee Milligan, who I still see to this very day. We've been friends for forty years, and he's worked with me throughout that time. He obviously saw in me some potential, and so he took it upon himself to lobby the board of directors at the club to allow me to use a cart.

Despite Lee's efforts my situation looked rather bleak. It seemed that a lock-solid rejection was on its way. Carts were just frowned upon at that time, and the logic was that if you were a golfer, you walked the course. Otherwise, you did not play the game, especially at my age.

However, Lee returned with a favorable verdict. How did he do it, I wondered. He told me that he simply made a great presentation to the board of directors, and they bought into the idea of this thirteen-year-old playing golf even if it meant using a cart. He said that he convinced them that they would be helping someone with great potential who truly loved the game of golf.

I threw myself into golf with unbounded enthusiasm. I often wonder now whether my doctor actually played golf. If he truly had played the game with the zeal that most physicians do today, he would have known that golf was extremely stressful on the knees, but just not to the same extent as football or the other major sports. However, because of Lee Milligan and a golf cart, I was able to walk ten yards to the ball, hit it, then walk back to the cart and take off to the next shot.

Golf became one of the most important things in my life at this time because it made me feel "normal." Feeling normal made me feel good about myself; it brought out my positive thinking and my happy personality. The game was an oasis for me, which I could retreat to any time life became tough and unbearable, whether it be from being teased or from being alone.

By the time I was a freshman in high school, my bone disorder had dissipated. Whether it was because of my young age and maturing process or simply because the pressure had been taken off my knee in the critical growth year, allowing the proper blood flow to be reestablished, I was now fit to play any sport I desired. I did participate in a number of other sports—basketball, volleyball—however, my love for the game of golf won out. I felt that the game seemed to love me at a time when I needed that love; I didn't want to abandon the very thing that had afforded me a sense of normalcy in my life when I desperately needed it.

I enjoy telling this story because it's typical of what happens in life. When I was thirteen, what seemed like the most devastating thing that could have happened turned out to be one of the greatest things that ever happened to me. Too often people get so focused on the problems that they're having that they can't seem to move through them, but if they do, something great may come out of it. I read stories of men who are forty-five or fifty years old and have mild heart attacks and then change their lifestyle and start exercising and eating properly and go on to have forty or fifty great years after that heart attack.

It's amazing now when I think back to those days of solitude in my room. There was this empty feeling that I wouldn't be perceived as normal. I can see myself as clear as day, sitting in my room and crying my eyes out after learning of my condition. Ironically, now I can honestly say it was one of the most auspicious things to ever happen to me. However, one result of overcoming adversity is that it usually forces a person to mature more quickly and think beyond his or her years. This happened to me, so I viewed the world differently from other kids. Thus my childhood illness, which at first was perceived by me and everyone around me as a tragedy, gave me a great perspective on golf and on life itself.

2. Growing Up

As a teenager growing up in Wisconsin I would spend the whole day at the golf course when I wasn't in school. My dad would meet me at 4:30 in the afternoon after work during the week in the summer, and we'd play nine holes of golf. It was a lot of fun. Dad and I had golf in common, and I can't tell you the number of times we'd arrive home at nine o'clock at night and have to reheat dinner. Mom understood and always managed to keep her smile, even though we were hours late for dinner.

As I said earlier, I was on crutches for a while and if you were to ask my father he would still get choked up to this day about how introverted I became because of feeling "different." Kids can be quite mean to each other, and a lot of my friends abandoned me, leaving only a few close ones to stay by my side.

When I would ride a cart at a tournament the folks there thought I was some pampered rich kid, not realizing that I was using the cart because of an illness. Many times if people can't see an illness with their eyes, they don't understand and they don't give anyone the benefit of the doubt.

Until my bone disease my life was just as routine as anyone else's life. I played kick the can, hide-and-seek, football, baseball, basketball, hockey—you name it, we played it. Life was good as a kid, but the bone disease changed everything. By then I was off the crutches, and because I'd played a heck of a lot of golf the summer before I entered high school, I entered many tournaments. Though I did not win a significant number of competitions, I shot a 72 on the second day in the city junior championships and I won that tournament. This was the best score I had ever shot and it was a big deal at that time.

My dad always supported my love of golf, but he was also an educator at heart and understood the need to do well in school. In junior high I had "citizenship" as a grade on my report card. Back then you had civics and not social studies and the courses had different titles. We were having supper and it was report card time. My dad was talking to me and I asked him if he regarded himself as a good citizen. He looked at me and said the proverbial yes. I asked him if he took his civic duties seriously and he said yes. "Good, because I got a C in citizenship," I announced to him. He suddenly was not very pleased. Nevertheless, he overlooked it and was still proud of me, anyway, but I tell the story because even though a parent can be proud of their children, they want to see them do well in school and they're disappointed when they bring home that type of grade.

The nicest times I've ever had on the golf course were when I was younger and was playing with my father. It's so difficult for parents to talk to their children about anything, but if you're on the golf course for four hours, there's a pretty good chance you and your mother or father will talk about something important. I've told an awful lot of dads to play golf with their children and to use it as a time to have a heart-to-heart talk with them.

Our spring trips to different golf courses in neighboring states were exciting. They were really golf adventures. When the lingering winter snows finally washed themselves away in spring's sunny skies, the adventures started. My basketball season was over, and so Friday

Getting ready for the big game

nights were free for my father and I to go on some great weekend excursions, arriving home late Sunday night just in time for me to get to bed and go to school on Monday. We'd drive to Memphis, Tennessee, and to southern Illinois. For us driving two hundred miles south was a breeze and we'd arrive late Friday night or early Saturday morning. We'd get a few hours' sleep and then play thirty-six holes of golf on Saturday. After an exhausting day we'd do the whole thing again on Sunday, playing thirty-six holes of golf and then driving back home late at night.

I was always nervous about playing tournaments in front of my parents, and so they'd drive me to the tournament, drop me off, and then pick me up afterward. However, the Western Junior, which was held in Bloomington, Indiana, was a trip on which my parents could not accompany me until the weekend, but I would have to make the cut. I shot a 69 on Monday and I called my dad to tell him I was in great shape. Then came Tuesday and I shot a 71. I missed the final 64 by one shot. I called my parents and they couldn't come and get me because it was in the middle of the week, so I had to take the bus home. When I got home the first thing I said to them was, "I'm not missing any more cuts because that bus ride home wasn't so good."

My relationship with Lee Milligan has lasted a lifetime. To this very day Lee lets me call him at home and he gives me instruction when I need it most. He was the golf professional at the Nakoma Golf

Club in Wisconsin, and then he left to become the golf professional at Barrington Hills Country Club in Illinois. My father and Lee both understood athletics and both saw the same vision in me: that I had what it took to be a professional golfer when I grew up. Thus, I had two sets of eyes watching over me, which was a comforting feeling. I knew everyone cared about me and I took this with me out on the golf course.

When Lee moved to Illinois I thought at first that it might hurt my game, but he had me visit with him on numerous occasions so that he was still able to coach me. More important than the lessons he gave me were the lessons he had me watch. He allowed me to watch him instruct other pupils. This was how I perfected my golf swing. I observed the faults and good swings of others and it helped me tremendously. I finally was able to understand my own golf swing and what worked well for me and what did not. I had a good foundation, which included as far as I was concerned a good grip, a good stroke, and a good short game.

I met Manuel de la Torre, a renowned teacher in Wisconsin, who works with Tommy Aaron on the SENIOR PGA TOUR today, and he and Lee had been good friends since their association on the Caribbean tour. Manuel changed my grip. He wanted me to weaken my grip and hit the entire bag of golf balls, hitting "the bag." I was supposed to hit the golf bag itself to get the feeling of a weakened grip. However, I hit the bag so hard I made a hole in it. Here was this beautiful kangaroo shag bag and I ruined it. Needless to say I felt terrible, but aside from ruining this great teacher's bag I came away from the experience with two important lessons. First, I had found my natural grip. Second, Lee wasn't afraid to go ask other great teachers for ideas and advice about what to do in certain situations. This was why I have always said that Lee Milligan was a great player and a great teacher. He also had a terrific short game, and I learned my entire chipping game by watching him.

Dad had spent so much time with Lee during my lessons that he knew when I was doing something wrong. Dad helped me a great deal when I played in high school because he was trained to look at me from a mechanical standpoint and told me what I was doing wrong, whether it was with my use of irons or with my chipping or putting.

High school golf in Wisconsin was always an adventure. The weather is cold and it's not really conducive to golf. It would be cold, windy, and really bad outside, and if you shot 36 in a nine-hole high school golf match, you'd kill everyone else. The weather was the X factor. The weather was so extreme that I would leave home in the morning and it would be great, but by the time my match started that afternoon the cold front would have dropped the temperature thirty degrees. And there I would be in my short sleeve shirt, freezing to death. This makes for interesting games of golf.

One great golf moment during my early years happened while my parents were out of the country, leaving them to read about my win. I would have loved them to be able to have seen it, but golf was not broadcast then as it is today. The Western Amateur was a prestigious tournament, and I was playing when my parents were in Brazil. Back then, when you left the United States, ESPN did not go with you. They couldn't see me on television or even get a radio report. They had to go to the U.S. embassy in Brazil just to read the *Wall Street Journal* sports score to find out how I was doing. I ended up winning the tournament and I made the *Wall Street Journal* again, which was the only way my parents knew that I won. I guess I gave them something nice to think about on the plane coming home.

One of my formidable opponents throughout junior high and high school was Jeff Radder. We went to different schools, but we would always be playing against each other, and one year we decided that one of us would enter the junior tournament and the other would enter the men's division. The year was 1967, and Jeff had won the big tournament at the junior level the year before. At that time he had been dominating the entire Wisconsin area, and the Midwest for that matter, with me giving him a run for it many times. I had also won my share of major tournaments, so we both received some great press coverage.

I played in the men's division and he ended up playing the junior division again. He won another junior title and I lost in the men's division. However, the real lesson here is that I elevated my game. It took my opponent the final hole of match play to beat me. The moral to the story is never give up, no matter what, because you just never know what can happen if things start clicking.

It was my sophomore year in high school and we were playing for the high school state championship. I had tweaked my neck a few days before the tournament and, even after some rest, it was still hurting me. I even went so far as to visit with a chiropractor, who gave me an adjustment on my neck. When the tournament finally started I was feeling better physically, but the weather was horrible.

This should be no surprise as the weather in the Midwest in the spring is usually unpredictable from morning to afternoon, much less from day to day. The first day was a crummy day, as the weather was rainy, cold, and windy, and my round was not so good, or so I thought. I shot a 79 and was quite upset with myself. I figured that my chances of having any type of comeback were slim. Before I knew it, it was the following morning already, as if the previous night flew right by, and round two was on my heels.

Low and behold that day I came out and I shot a 73 and had a great day two, despite awful weather once again. At the end of the two-day event, I wound up tied for the lead, so there was a playoff. I ended up winning the high school state championship in a playoff.

It just goes to prove my point that you should never give up because you never know what's going to happen. I didn't think I'd get to play at all because of my injury, much less to tie and to play in a playoff and then to win. I won the tournament again the following year, and this was the start of my golf rollercoaster ride, with the best yet to come.

I also loved the game of basketball and have always loved it. My love of basketball is a direct reflection on our school system here in Wisconsin, at least back in my time. They started us in organized sports in third grade. I had after-school team practice, and we even played games against other schools in a competitive manner starting in the third grade. This is unheard of today, but back then sports were king. There was an elementary school team, a junior high school team, and a high school team. It was the game to watch, and back then Monona was a huge sports town. I had my own sports routine when I was a little kid. I would play football in the fall, basketball in the winter, golf and baseball in the spring and summer. I enjoy watching college hoops to this day, and I wear my Wisconsin cap whenever the team is in the NCAA tournament. I really take a lot of pride in my basketball-playing days in high school, after my bone disease had dissipated. I was one of the starters on my basketball team and was six three in high school as a freshman. Basketball did not interfere with my golf game, and so I could play both sports.

I went to Florida to play in this golf tournament and all of the long hours of being out in the hot sun gave me this great tan. Well, I thought it was a great tan, until I came back to Wisconsin. All the girls made fun of me. I looked ridiculous in my basketball tank top. I was the only one on the basketball court with a deep tan, and even when we traveled the visiting teams and fans made fun of me. My own future wife, Susan, made fun of me.

I continued to play varsity basketball, but my love for golf was just a bit greater. I had to choose at some point between these two sports, so I chose golf because I felt that it was within my sights to turn professional. My junior year in high school was a good basketball year for me, but a better golf year, as I shot 67 in the final round of the high school tournament to win. I soon only focused my attention on national golf events during that summer of my junior year. I traveled all over the country and enjoyed it all.

I had a terrific senior year in high school, playing in the state tournaments on my varsity volleyball team. One of the reasons why I played volleyball was because I thought we could win at it, and we did. The other reason I chose to play volleyball was because the game is a great way in which to improve your basketball game. The jumping and the timing of shots that take place in volleyball forces you, I believe, to be a better basketball player.

My senior year in high school saw me become captain of my basketball team, set scoring records for the high school, and become an all-conference; all-state in the state of Wisconsin. However, no sport won my heart like golf. The game of golf was just special to me and it was something that I knew, deep inside me, that I wanted to pursue as a career. I was captain of my golf team as well, and it was special to me. People ask me if I am glad I chose to play golf over basketball and I always say if I had it to do over again, I'd make the same decisions.

I was fortunate to have been recruited by some of the best schools in the country. My high school academic and sports record gave me the opportunity to travel and meet various college golf coaches, but the one coach whom I liked the most was the coach at the University of Florida—Buster Bishop. He told it like it was, not what I wanted to hear. How I met Coach Bishop is another great story. Buster and I formally met at the Orange Bowl in Miami and he impressed me a great deal. I was in Miami for the Orange Bowl junior golf tournament, which was held around Christmastime. It was a tournament that drew young high school golfers from all over the world. It truly was a global tournament, and an important one, and Buster happened to be there at the same time and he spoke with me about the University of Florida, but not as a salesman for the university. He spoke to me in a very real manner, and there was something genuine and special about Buster that attracted me to learning more about this school and its golf program.

Although I was young and impressionable, I just had this sense and vision that Buster Bishop would be the right coach at the right college for me. I knew I could trust him to always be honest with me and he always was, which is why to this day I'll go play golf with him and my father down in Florida. I could tell which coaches were honest and which ones were just feeding me lines. He cared about the players, recruiting athletes who were great players and great students.

Coach Bishop coached both for life on the course and for life off the course. Most of the players have stayed in touch with him over the years. I still see him regularly and I play golf with him when I go through Gainesville. He's in his seventies, and he's still wound up as tight as can be and it's terrific.

The summer before I left home for college was interesting. I qualified for the National Amateur and was the lowest qualifier in the country that year, shooting 12 under par in a thirty-six-hole regional qualifier in Oconomowoc. I went to Columbus, Ohio, for the tournament and missed the cut. This was discouraging, but it was a good way to get started and cap off the summer and get ready for college.

College was the best yet to come for me. I loved college and I'm so glad I finished school and had those magical years at the University of Florida. One of the other aspects of the University of Florida that I liked was the great weather. They had a great business school and the whole package attracted me. At the time Florida had won the National Championship in golf the year before I arrived. College was a whole different ball game than high school, however. Choosing the right school is one of the most important decisions any youngster makes in his or her life.

Although that first day of college was interesting, I spent the entire first week running around adding and dropping courses. The summers were also incredible, as my buddies and I would have our golf excursions, and I got to take my dad's Cadillac! My love of cars was just at its infancy here. Little did I know I would become one of the ultimate car nuts.

I struggled with golf in college because in Florida the grass is Bermuda grass. Bermuda is coarse and grainy, which affects ball flight, whereas the grass in the Midwest is *bent*. When the Florida winds kicked up their heels, my balls just took off as if never to return. I wasn't playing well until I started to figure out the grass and how not to hit the ball too high . . . One of the tougher adjustments that I had to make when I started playing golf in college was getting used to Bermuda grass, merely because I hadn't played much on courses that used it.

The key in playing Bermuda grass is getting used to the change of speeds in the greens. The fairways are not a problem because they don't differ too much from other types of fairways. The two problems with Bermuda grass lie with the rough and with the greens. The Bermuda greens tend to be faster down grain and slower into the grain. That means that a ball hit down grain will take off faster from the moment of impact with the club head. On the other hand, a ball putted into the grain of the green will travel slower. Unfortunately the only secret to mastering this type of green was practice. There wasn't anything I could change with regard to my stance or swing. I had to keep practicing and after a while it became second nature to me.

As for getting out of Bermuda rough, where the ball tends to become embedded, the only answer is practice. After a while you can feel your way out of any type of golf course rough. I compare the Bermuda grass situation with myself to that of a baseball player who goes from playing on natural grass his entire childhood at public parks to playing at college on Astroturf, or differently manicured grass. You just need some time to adjust to it. Time and practice often take care of everything.

Every coach has a personality that enables them to be a coach. It's not as if they just walked onto a college campus and started coaching. Coach Bishop had been a football coach and, being an exceptional golfer, he decided to coach golf. He did an outstanding job, and the main reason for his success was that he knew how to teach and how to best illustrate his points. He knew how to demonstrate the use of a five iron to chip and he knew how to tell us what we were doing wrong. However, his one idiosyncrasy was his penchant for punctuality.

Punctuality could have been labeled as part of the college curriculum when it came to Buster. You could not be late with Buster, not ever! If he told you that the team was leaving at eight o'clock in the morning and you showed up at eight o'clock in the morning, he was already gone. To Buster eight o'clock in the morning meant quarter to eight. He was not going to be late for anything or anyone on principle. He left players behind. He thought that if you didn't care enough to be there fifteen minutes early, you did not care enough to go on the trip. It didn't matter who the players were, he would leave players and he left our stars behind. However, I feel that this has stood me in good stead for life. I had always been a punctual kid in school and his strong feelings about being on time made a lasting impression on me and my teammates. The guys really loved playing for him, as he treated everyone equally. He also knew how to have fun with us, knowing we were young and had that competitive spirit in us.

We were playing the Miami Invitational and before that tournament started Coach Bishop made us a proposition. Talk about extra incentive, this deal was the best one ever. He promised us that if we won by forty shots, he would give each and every player two dozen golf balls. However, if we won, but only by less than forty shots, then each player had to give him two dozen golf balls. After the third round we were ahead of the other teams by twenty-nine shots. All the guys were clapping and hollering and it was great. Coach Bishop really enjoyed watching us celebrate prematurely. Then came the eighteenth hole.

There I was on the par 4 eighteenth hole on the final round and I needed a birdie to give us exactly a forty-shot victory. All eyes were on me and it was an electric feeling. I had hit a very good tee shot and my second shot was also a very good shot, which landed on the green about ten feet from the cup. Even Coach Bishop was rooting me on, and I laughed and stepped aside for a second from the shot. No one in the crowd knew about this inside incentive plan. I took Coach Bishop aside and I said to him, "I'm gonna knock it right down in the back of that cup." To which he replied, "You're gonna miss the shot and it's gonna cost you," and he laughed. I stood over that putt and knocked it right back in the back of that cup just as I had guaranteed. It cost Coach Bishop ten dozen golf balls!

When it came to grudge matches one school really got us peaked for top performance: the University of Houston. They were our most formidable opponent, a terrific golf school with a phenomenal team during my college years. It just so happened that our schools locked up in some momentous competitions during my college days. Dave Williams was in charge of the golf team for the University of Houston. Coach Bishop would always rent two station wagons whenever we would go down and play them in Texas. The wagons were comfortable, as we used them to get from the airport to the motel, and from the motel to the golf course. Well, I was so sure we would clean up that I told Coach Bishop, "We're going to need another wagon just to take all of those trophies home!" Sure enough, at the tournament's end, we cleaned up. We took, with the exception of one trophy, the entire trophy table home with us. We must have won more than forty different trophies and it seemed as if I was a little Joe Namath guaranteeing victories. I had backed up my pre-tournament comments with great play throughout and Coach Bishop got a big kick out of seeing us load up that wagon with all of those trophies. You can't possibly imagine what a 1970 station wagon full of trophies looks like until you see it filled to the maximum with these big trophies, much less dozens of them.

Traveling in college on team trips was a heck of a lot of fun. Then there was Albuquerque, New Mexico, and the Albuquerque Invitational. It was a great golf tournament and a great golf course. For me, however, my biggest opponent was my own putting game. Coach Bishop observed this firsthand as he walked out on the ninth hole and saw me standing there on the green, waiting to putt. I began to take my putting stroke and Coach later told me that he couldn't believe what he was seeing. What he saw, instead of me using my normal putting stroke, was a young man so bent over it looked as if his putter was broken. In fact, he was convinced the putter's shaft had broken off. It was only after he saw the slight backstroke I made that he realized he might be wrong about me having a broken putter. When I hit the ball and he saw my putter was intact, he was amazed.

He turned to me and he said, "Andrew, have you changed your putting style?" "Yes, Coach, I'm experimenting because my putting ain't worth anything," I told him. I was experimenting with a new putter I had purchased for two dollars, and it changed my life. I became very comfortable with that putter and I perfected a unique technique of choking up on it so much that it looked as if the putter was broken and I was trying to hold the two halves of it together with my hands.

Although I remember his aghast look, I also remember Coach was quite pleased with my new and improved results. What drove me to buy this putter in the first place was that I was at my wit's end with regard to my putting. Nothing worked for me. I thought that if I didn't need improvement, then I should be almost perfect on the green, and I wasn't at all. Improvement, many times, comes with self-evaluation and change, and I thought it was time to change putters and try something new. Even in baseball, batters experiment with their stances. A Hall of Fame hitter such as Cal Ripken, Jr., has experimented over the years with his stance.

College golf in 1971 was a lot of fun for me, as I had newfound confidence in my own game, and I had a lot of great head-to-head competitions. Ben Crenshaw and I were the two best players in the country that year. There was such an incredible amount of golf talent scattered all around that it was one of the best college years ever. It was one of my best school years and I loved every minute of it. At the University of Florida with me were players I was proud to call teammates, such as Steve Melnyk, Gary Koch, Andy Bean, Mike Killian, Fred Ridley. Then there was the incredible dynamic duo at the University of Texas: Tom Kite and Ben Crenshaw. Wake Forest University had its own prodigies in Eddie Pierce and Lanny Wadkins. The University of Arizona was lucky to have Don Pooley. Howard Twitty and Mark Hayes; and Doug Tewell were at Oklahoma State cleaning up, and Tom Watson was at Stanford University ready to break out onto the scene the next year and turn professional.

That year was so great that we had an impromptu reunion at the Tucson Open in 1996. Tucson was the site of the greatest of memories for us. We played the NCAA Championship there in 1971 and it was the twenty-fifth anniversary of that championship season. There were twenty golfers who played in the NCAA Tournament in 1971 who were still playing in that tournament in Tucson as PGA TOUR players in 1996! Can you believe that? It's incredible when you think about that particular pool of talent and how many of my young comrades went on to have illustrious golfing careers. Coach Bishop feels much about that year as I do, that it was a magical one in college golf history.

One of the biggest events in college other than the NCAA Championship was the 1971 Houston Intercollegiate. It was a tournament run by Dave Williams, the coach at Houston, the host team. The rules were changed to benefit the Houston team. I'm serious. He would allow substitutions in the middle of a tournament because he had extra players. You could be playing, and this happened to us, and there were three guys from the University of Houston having a playoff to see who would play the next day.

Golf gave me normalcy at a time when I desperately needed it.

The tournament would have many pairings and little battles going on, but the events were weighted based on how his team was faring. If his guys were doing better in the two-man teams, then that became more important than the individual matches. It's funny how lopsided it was and how important the tournament was to schools around the country. I won the tournament that year individually. Gary Koch and I beat Tom Kite and Ben Crenshaw to win the two-man team and to win the tournament for our school. Coach was not there because he was ill, and so the victory was even sweeter because we got to take the trophy back to him. We won it for our coach, and against Crenshaw and Kite. Looking back now I realize how sweet it was for Gary and me to beat Tom and Ben. Crenshaw and Kite are two of the top golfers of all time, but that week belonged to us.

Winning the Western Amateur and finishing second at the Porter Cup were two great experiences for me at the end of college, seeing the countryside and winning. My senior year in college I won some tournaments, but my focus was on turning professional and getting married. Some of the excitement of college golf was waning for me. I was now setting my sights on the pro circuit. We didn't win the NCAA my final year, and it was disappointing that I was not a member of an NCAA championship team. The University of Florida, as a school, won the year before I came, and the year after I left. I thought that three of the four years that I was there our teams were better than the other two winning teams. Once I graduated, I turned professional and got married. I played in tournaments in Tampa with Gary McCord and Tom Kite. We were all preparing for Q-school that fall.

Although Tom and Gary and I practiced together, I was married and had my own life outside golf, and they were trying to start their own lives outside of golf. Golf, unlike team sports, doesn't give players much of a chance to hang around together off the course. A group of young golfers might play practice rounds together and might have a great time in the clubhouse together, but there is no "home town" atmosphere because the cities change from week to week. I often found myself wanting to spend more time with my wife, Susan, when I was not on the golf course, as did the other players with their respective families.

3. My First PGA TOUR Victory: Westchester

Television often places an enormous amount of emphasis on the majors. It's almost as if they're saying, "Win a major. Be a king for a year!" If you lose, people question what type of year you had, as they do to the teams that come up short in the playoffs in baseball and basketball. Needless to say, however, that I myself was one of those kids who always thought that winning a major would mean everything. The majors were the tournaments that I held as a goal for myself when I was young.

"If I could reach the majors and be competitive," I'd often tell myself, "I'd be on top of the world." The U.S. Open was one of the most storied majors, and there was always a great deal of golf drama surrounding every single U.S. Open tournament.

Winning majors such as the U.S. Open, however, doesn't just happen to you overnight. It's not as if one fine day you wake up and suddenly you can play golf better than the number one player in the world. In my book you have to make U.S. Open wins happen by establishing the necessary building blocks along the way. Life is a journey and the end is never as enjoyable as the journey. The journey, to me, is life, not just the means to get somewhere.

After college and once I reached the professional level, I saw the majors as more within my grasp. I knew that if I could ever win a major it would always mean something to me, even fifty years later!

As a kid, I had always dreamed of winning a Masters or U.S. Open and 1978 seemed like it would be my year to establish myself as a young golfer who could win the big one.

I went through the Q-school in the fall of 1972, and at the year's end I missed qualifying at the Heritage in Hilton Head, but I made the cut at Disney, which got me into the L.A. Open the following year. I played the Snowball Open, a small regional tourney, with my college roommate Stacy Russell, the week afterward in Lexington, Kentucky, for something to do and I won that tournament. All of a sudden I had another check under my belt and it was great. The next year I thought would be great for me. I was on top of my game, and if I had stayed amateur I would have played on the Walker Cup team that summer. I made the decision because I didn't want to miss that year's Q-school and possibly end up two years behind everyone else. The decision made a lot of sense to me, as some of my friends chose the Walker Cup and regretted it because they missed Q-school for another year. I wanted to get on with my life as an adult.

Susan and I drove out to Los Angeles from Gainesville, Florida, for the Los Angeles Open. I was going to play the West Coast swing for about six or seven weeks. The very first hole of my first event in my first full year as a pro golfer was a disaster! I hit a snap hook out of bounds on a par-5 hole that could have been reached in two shots. I looked bad—really bad. My second tee shot also went out of bounds. The third shot was another bad hook but at least it was in bounds. I finally got the ball on the green and in the hole to finish my first hole that year with a double-bogy seven! I shot 75 that day and wanted my amateur status back. I went from feeling that I didn't belong to making the cut and being paired with Arnold Palmer on Saturday and hoping that I did belong on tour.

One of my huge mistakes as a rookie was playing eighteen tournaments in a row! I was so tired that I just didn't play well. Although everyone was telling me to take a week off I didn't listen to anyone. I kept at it because I was twenty-two and inexperienced and determined, and it took its toll on my confidence. Everything I thought that continuous play would do for me, the opposite happened. I thought I'd get better, and instead I got worse. I missed the top 60 by a few thousand dollars and it was disappointing. There was a rule back then that if golfers finished in the top 25 of an event they were in that event next year. I did manage to finish in the top 25 a few times, so I only had to endure a Monday-morning qualifier once the following year. I was able to manage my schedule a lot more, and I constantly improved each year.

Although I played well in the PGA Championship in 1975, finishing fourth, and I qualified for the U.S. Open at Medina, I played halfway decently in the 1975 U.S. Open, finishing twelfth. I knew that I wasn't quite there yet. I always felt that my game was suited to major championships and that my game was progressing as a player, but I needed something to lift my spirits. In 1976 I had many top-10 finishes. Even though I did not win a tournament in 1976, I was in great shape with enough top-10 finishes.

The first time I drove up Magnolia Drive at the Masters was breathtaking. The year was 1976. History was everywhere. All of the things I had read and heard about seemed to come to life. The most nervous during that entire week at the Masters was on Wednesday afternoon, playing in the par-3 tournament. This is a wonderful par-3, nine-hole course, that they play every year on Wednesday afternoon to try and relax everyone. The first hole is a seventy-yard shot and the green is about forty feet by thirty feet. The green is totally surrounded by fans, and all I could think about was that I was scared I'd kill someone. I imagined this horrific sight of hitting someone in the head with an errant shot. I was fine after I hit my first shot and managed not to kill anyone. The first hole on Thursday was not nearly as nerve-racking as it was that Wednesday. It's rather incredible that I was not as nervous when play actually counted as when everyone was just fooling around. I ended up shooting 66 the first round of my first Masters. I was on top of the world and Raymond Floyd shot 65. I thought I could win the Masters that week. That changed in a hurry. I shot 81 the second day! I learned that day that if you are a tiny bit off-line at Augusta National, you are going to pay for it. I had the ball on the wrong side of the hole the entire second day, but I made the cut.

In 1977 I won my first tournament at Westchester at age twenty-seven. This was just what the golf doctor ordered. I finally felt that my golf game had progressed and I had confidence in myself going into 1978. However, Westchester did not look promising for me at the beginning of the ProAm.

Little did I know in the spring of 1977 that the Westchester Country Club in Rye, New York, would be the place where I would finally collect my first win as a professional PGA TOUR player. Up until that point in the season I had played reasonably well at times, but a month or so before I had struggled mightily with pain. My back and neck were both bothering me to the point where I was traveling with a portable traction device whereby I could hang in my room at night for thirty minutes at a time.

The idea behind the portable traction machine was to help alleviate the spasms in my neck. This is the kind of stuff that gets treated very easily nowadays, but twenty-five years ago medicine was quite different from an orthopedic standpoint. There just wasn't much help out there for me, and so I tried everything. I did whatever I could and saw whatever physician I could to help temper the pain. I had missed three cuts prior to Westchester, all because of a bad neck and back. I had missed the cut at the PGA at Pebble Beach right before Westchester and flew to Napa, California, and played in a two-day ProAm. I played so horribly that I called Susan, who had already flown to New York, to tell her that I was going home. She said, "Not on your life!"

She wanted to attend plays and do shopping in New York. I ended up taking the red-eye from San Francisco to New York and arrived that Wednesday morning. I played in the ProAm with Dan Rostenkowski, Tip O'Neill, Jamie Whitten, and Howard Evans, a highly ranked vice president of JC Penney at the time. We played nine holes, got rained out, sat around all afternoon and just talked. I had shot 40 on the first nine holes. Stewart Klein, the gentleman that sponsored this group, helped support me. He had guaranteed Tip O'Neill that Dave Stockton would play in the group, because Tip liked Stockton. Instead, they played with a new kid on tour—me. However, they loved the fact that I had lunch with them and talked all day. It all ended well, and Tip and I had a great time. It also began a nice friendship for us.

I went out on Thursday, round one, and strange things happened to me. I hit some great shots and played a terrific front nine, and a good back nine. I repeated my great stroke the very next day on Friday and on Saturday shot a 65 to lead the tourney. The year before at Kings Island I had been leading, but Ben Crenshaw stepped up his game and beat me. I was not about to let that happen again. I wanted my first victory and knew that it was within my sights before the start of play on Sunday morning. Sunday was very windy. I knew, given the layout of Westchester, that the wind would play an important factor and that it would be an extremely arduous task to shoot a really low score. I ended up playing well and winning my first professional tournament. Susan and Nichole, my oldest daughter, were there, and Nichole came running onto the eighteenth green after I won. It was a cool moment, and I have some great pictures to relive that moment each day.

4. The 1978 U.S. Open

It was 1978 and I had finished second in the Tournament of Champions. I had finished second at Kemper a few weeks before the Open. Kemper was the last tournament I played before the U.S. Open, and I'd had that winning feeling.

After Kemper I even took the week off because I thought that the extra rest before the Open would do wonders for me. The plan was for me to fly to Denver the week before. We had a family cookout at the house that weekend. Unfortunately for me I had eaten some pork that had not been cooked through enough, and I got violently ill with food poisoning. Here my dream week turned into a week in bed. Instead of getting extra rest and being all ready for the practice rounds, I had to get over the sweats and fever in four days and then fly to Denver just to make it there in time for the start of the week.

I ended up flying out on Saturday, and I stayed with my friend Tom Babb, a golf professional in Denver. I even performed a clinic and exhibition that Sunday and felt as if things were going well. I also felt that this helped in acclimating me to the high altitude, as well as helping to get me in the right frame of mind for the tournament. When I first looked at Cherry Hills I saw this easy-looking, not really long, course. It didn't look tricky to me, and I knew that the altitude wouldn't be a problem. I changed my mind rather quickly about the course when I played it. The fairways were fast, and the rough was plentiful, making it crucial to hit the fairway.

The practice rounds at Cherry Hills on Monday, Tuesday, and Wednesday came and went all too quickly, and my game was nowhere near where it should have been if I was to emerge on Sunday with a victory. I really didn't have much confidence in myself. I couldn't hit the ball solidly at all. As a professional golfer you know how your body feels when you're going to win and you know if something isn't right. I just knew something wasn't right inside of me. Unfortunately there was no time left for practice or for any development of a routine. It was Thursday, round one, and it was showtime for me.

I teed-off that Thursday without the confidence that a winner would have on his tee-off shot, and the result was a towering drive right down the heart of the first fairway. I couldn't fathom this whole situation at all. My drive was terrific, as if I had practiced as usual, but I hadn't. The lost time obviously hadn't hindered my game, at least not on that first drive. I might have been ill, but when it counted on Thursday, round one, I produced.

I had often heard the story of the 1960 U.S. Open, when Arnold Palmer drove the ball on the first green that Saturday, since they didn't play on Sundays back then, and he electrified the crowd. He birdied five of the first six holes and ended up winning the whole tournament.

I tried to drive the ball onto the green, just like Arnold, but couldn't. There's no way you can drive it onto the green from the tee nowadays, as it was redesigned. Interestingly enough, Arnold Palmer was brought in to help redesign the first tee, and he made sure that no one could hit it onto the first green!

It was now time for my second shot and I decided, based on my lie, to hit a wedge. My swing felt like it was in sync, and my wedge shot was a good one. Everything leading up to the striking of the ball with the club face feels comfortable and is in rhythm.

I continued to hit the ball very well all day long, finishing with a 70 for Thursday, to go one under for the tournament. Hale Irwin led after the first day with a two-under 69, and here I was in a comfortable second place. I even ran into someone that day who made me feel good about myself. Life, like golf, is often a tournament, with a lot of even more interesting side stories.

There was a gentleman running the press tent by the name of Johnny Dee. I wondered if this could be the same person who was the former basketball coach at Notre Dame, whom I had spoken to coming out of high school regarding the possibility of playing basketball there. I had not seen him since my senior year in high school. It was indeed the same man, and we had a nice, friendly meeting in the press room. We talked about college and my future in golf, and it really relaxed me to know he was there rooting me on—my own little gallery.

My partners the first two days were Dale Douglas and Leonard Thompson, both great guys and both of whom were friends. I played well on Friday, shooting another round of 70. This time my 70 gave me the lead. As I said, as in life itself, in golf there are many subplots and here's another side story.

The last time the U.S. Open was played at Cherry Hills, Arnold Palmer had won. I had made a thirty-five-foot birdie putt on the eighteenth hole to take the lead on Friday. If I had two-putted, Arnold Palmer would have made the cut and played the weekend. However, by making that putt, Arnold was cut out of the weekend. This did not sit well with the usual throng of fans who came to cheer Arnold Palmer. Although the fans didn't personally blame me for this disaster, they were probably not happy with me making that putt. The biggest name in golf was cut out of the weekend all because of my putt, as a result of the ten-shot rule. If the leader goes out and shoots really low, you can eliminate many guys making the cut. By not parring the hole, but by making birdie on the last hole with a great thirty-five-foot putt, Arnold Palmer and many of my friends missed the cut. The putt actually broke about eight feet. Although I wanted to see Arnold play, like everyone else, I was happy with my position in the tournament.

I was paired with Jack Nicklaus on Saturday. This was a dream pairing for me, and I was determined to have fun with it. Just playing with Jack was enjoyable. He was so great to me as a young player that the experience just made me feel as if I belonged there, as if I belonged on the PGA TOUR. I started to really understand what Jack was all about from the walk to the very first hole. I remember walking to that first tee and looking over at him in total awe and I actually said to him, "Hey, play well." He just laughed because he couldn't believe that anyone would speak to him and wish *him* luck at the first tee.

There were many times during that third round where Jack had skillfully landed his ball on the green within two feet of the hole. Instead of tapping in and making that easy two-footer, with me either three feet away or fifteen feet away, Jack marked his ball each time and allowed me to putt. The rules clearly allow the person exceptionally close to the hole to hole out. This would have meant that Jack would have finished his putts and his gallery would have followed him. Thus, the swelling crowds would have hustled themselves away, and I would have been left with a ghost town, or with the noise of everyone rustling around to catch a glimpse of Jack on the next tee. Instead, Jack allowed me to finish my putts and we walked off each green together and strolled with the crowds to the next tee. After briefly losing the lead during the course of play, I made a long putt to take the lead once again by the day's end that Saturday. He made a great tee shot right down the middle of the fairway at the thirteenth hole and then went over to a restroom and after that was never the same. He dumped the second shot and ended up making a 7. He commented to me that he guessed he shouldn't have gone in the "little room." I had a solid round of golf, and I made a long birdie putt on the eighteenth hole, about a fifty-footer going up the hill. I felt confident and ready for all of the drama that was known to happen on Sunday. Generally I don't sleep well at any time. Lee Milligan had flown in to see me play. Lee and Tom, with whom I was staying, had worked together. I slept until 9:00 A.M. the next morning, after picking up Lee at the airport late that night. Maybe the sleep was good for me. Why I slept that late on a tournament day I still don't know, but it was a puzzling event because I have never slept later than 6:00 A.M. on any day, much less a tournament day, ever, except for that one day.

Sunday was to be the biggest day of my young golfing career. I was in complete control of what I was doing. My playing partner on Sunday was the great Gary Player, another icon of the game of golf. If I ever thought that I was decent at playing bunker shots, I was now paired with the bunker legend himself. Gary owned the "beach," and he could make getting out of the toughest bunkers look effortless. Once again, I was privileged to be playing with one of the men I adored and idolized. It was hard to keep from being in awe of him, but I told myself that if I was to ever win a major I would need to make it happen this very day. Gary's quest for his second U.S. Open victory, which would have given him at least two wins in all four majors, added to the excitement.

The day started on the right track, my tee shot went where I wanted it to go, and I seemed to be off to a real nice start on the front nine. The next thing I know, I have a four-shot lead going into thirteen. The thirteenth hole at Cherry Hills is a short par-4. I hit a decent drive down the fairway and followed up with a good iron shot. The pin was in a tough position: the back left corner of the green. I reached the green and had a fifteen-foot putt for a birdie. I told my caddie, Gary Crandall, that this tournament was mine. I relaxed and made that fifteen-foot putt for birdie.

I was now in control of the tournament with a five-stroke lead. I thought to myself that my chance of winning a major was in reach.

When I knocked the putt in to go five ahead, I thought it was the greatest event that had happened to me. However, it just might have been the worst thing that could have happened to me.

Getting into the psyche of a golfer is hard to explain, but sometimes your own mind plays tricks on you. When a golfer gets far ahead in a tournament the natural inclination is to think about the "lead" rather than about taking care of business on the last few holes. Not only did I not eat up the rest of the course, I didn't make one decent shot the rest of the way.

The fourteenth hole was proof that too much of a lead is not a good thing on Sunday. Lo and behold I made bogey at the fourteenth. The fifteenth hole was even worse for me. I made a double bogey at fifteen. I had hit an iron shot into the deep bunker along the way. In the meantime, I'm losing three shots. The sixteenth hole proved crucial for me. If I made just one more bogey or mistake, then the tournament would be up for grabs and I would be known as having one of the worst collapses on Sunday at the U.S. Open. I settled myself down and made par at 16. The seventeenth hole was another critical hole and I made yet another par at hole 17. The stage was now set for a real showdown on the eighteenth hole.

The eighteenth hole at Cherry Hills during the U.S. Open was a brutal par 4. It's a par 5 for the membership during year-round play, but the USGA converted it into a par 4 for the 1978 U.S. Open. The hole played about 480 yards, and uphill. To make matters even more worse for me, there is the infamous lake that runs along the entire left side of the hole. If you hit it left, you'd just have to re-tee. For me that would have meant losing the lead and probably losing the tournament. It's really hard finishing a hole on any day, much less when every shot is as critical as in a major. So here I am with this one-shot lead, and now I'm right where I dreamed of being as a kid. I kept thinking to myself, "Let's figure out a way to make par and win this championship."

I hit a three-iron off the tee; my thinking was just to hit it in the fairway, and it was a long drive. I must have hit that ball 270 yards. I absolutely killed it, but I hit it through the fairway slightly and into the rough. The lie was not very good to say the least, but J. C. Snead and Dave Stockton missed putts at 18, and now my lead had increased to two shots.

Suddenly my thinking changed. Instead of trying to do something stupid and desperate out of the rough, I told myself to just take out my eight-iron and try to get back on the fairway. The lake cut into the fairway, and so I had to hit the ball about 110 yards to carry the corner of the lake. The ball came out solidly and I hit it right down the fairway and left myself with a fifty-yard pitch shot, or sand-wedge shot, whichever I preferred, to the green.

As I was ready for the oh-so-crucial pitch shot, Mother Nature had different plans. I was ready to take my swing and the wind howled like mad. We're talking a thirty-five- or forty-mile-per-hour wind gust. All I had to do was get the ball on the green and two-putt to make bogie, and I'd win the U.S. Open. I hit the pitch shot perfectly. As the ball was traveling in the air my only concern was that it go past the hole. The eighteenth green at Cherry Hills slants dramatically from back to front. If you miss the green and you leave yourself with a pitch shot coming back, you will be in trouble. The wind was so strong that the ball got knocked down, came up short, and caught the top lip of the bunker, only to roll back down into it.

Now I've made it exciting for everyone for all the wrong reasons. The people in the gallery started moaning and groaning. I assessed the situation and thought that my sand wedge ought to do the trick. I winked at my caddie and said, "Let's see if I can get some points for bunker player of the year." I had always been a solid player in the sand, and the fact that I made this shot and put the ball on the green close to the hole really relaxed me. I ended up four feet short of the hole, a straight uphill putt. You couldn't have had the ball in a better position on the green if you set it there.

So now Gary Player finishes, and I'm left to make my four-foot putt to win the U.S. Open. I could not have had an easier putt under the circumstances. It was straight uphill, and I could be aggressive with it. Gary and I lined up the putt, and it was just a right-center putt. The wind was howling once again, and the ball looked as if it would be whisked away by the wind. I backed off. I then reapproached the ball and got myself set all over again to putt, and once again the wind swelled around me. Again I was stopped cold in my tracks. The crowd at this point became impatient with me, and they let me know it loud and clear, with their ooing, aahing, and comments. It wasn't that I thought I would choke and miss the putt. I wasn't afraid of the putt. I was just being cautious. The whole scene was quite a sight to behold, and describing it just doesn't do it justice. It's one of those sights and moments in sports you have to experience on the course as a player, not as a fan. I felt that once I touched that ball with my club, the wind would carry it away somewhere to another land. I once again backed off and hoped the wind would die.

For the third time I stood over the putt, and it was as if someone upstairs said, "Hey, it's your turn to win," and the wind stopped dead. I ended up knocking the putt in to win the U.S. Open. It was a great relief and the first person, other than the two Garys (Gary Player and Gary Crandall), to come over to congratulate me was Bob Rosburg, the ABC course commentator.

Bob walked over to me and said, "Man, am I glad you made it." I said, "Thanks, Rossie. I appreciate you pulling for me and it was really nice of you to care about me making this putt." "I didn't care about that," he interrupted. "If you'd have missed that putt we'd have a play-off tomorrow and for two good reasons I didn't want to do a playoff tomorrow. First, Eleanor, my wife, had you in her pool to win, and, second, I've got a corporate outing tomorrow." Here I was sweating to win the Open, and he's concerned about his wife's golf pool and his corporate outing. That's why I love this game. Only friends are that refreshingly honest with you. For me the win was worth a stamp on my career, and for Bob it was worth a bunch of money to him. I was not that shocked by my victory because of age and progress. I knew that my twenties would see me win one major, and I felt like this was the beginning of big things for me.

I finally got off the green and headed for the scorer's tent. After signing my scorecard and recording it with the officials in the tent, I headed for the press and stopped only to call home.

This was Father's Day. Susan was at home and was eight months pregnant with our second daughter. My oldest daughter, Nichole, was four years old at the time. She was not exactly watching golf when I called her. I, however, was still in my whirlwind frame of mind and was savoring my big day in golf history. I knew I had won and I had just signed my golf card. The celebration was all set. The USGA was getting ready to make the trophy presentation and I rushed into the tent to call my wife. Nichole answered the phone, as it should have been scripted on Father's Day, and she said, "Gee, Dad, Happy Father's Day!" My family really meant everything to me. I asked her if she got to watch any of it. She said, "I watched you for a few minutes and then mom got me one of those plastic pools and I've been in the pool all day!" Here I was having so much fun being a big shot winning the U.S. Open, and my daughter was in her little pool. Actually it was the best Father's Day message anyone could ever get, and it was the first of many such moments that helped to put golf, and its relationship with life in the real world, in perspective for me.

The entire week had so many neat memories, and it was something I truly appreciated. At the time I was twenty-eight years old, and I not only got to play with the great players of the game as partners, but I got the chance to win in front of them. I felt as if I was a Pinocchio of sorts and had proved myself to be a genuine professional in their eyes.

After my victory, some interesting things happened to me. Sometimes you make commitments early in the season without knowing your future schedule. I had committed myself to partake in an outing in Montreal, for the sponsor of the Canadian Open. The plane picked me up Sunday night right after I had won the U.S. Open, and we flew to Montreal. At the outing there were ten players, including Nicklaus, Palmer, Watson, and Trevino, and among them this young kid—me. Here I had won the major, and the dinner that they had for us was memorable because Arnold Palmer stood up and toasted me. Arnold stood up and raised his wineglass and said, "Gee, Andy, we would like to welcome you to this new club you joined yesterday of major winners." I looked around the table at all of these great players and I felt as if they were genuinely accepting me into their club. It was one of the best feelings I ever had in my life—being toasted by the legendary Arnold Palmer.

I had yet another golf outing to attend in Detroit the very next day. I flew into Detroit on Tuesday morning. The outing was benefiting the Police Athletic League to help raise money for kids in the Detroit area. Football legend Nightrain Lane ran this outing, and it was a lot of fun to show the youngsters some things about the game of golf. Then it was off to Florida for yet a third outing. I performed at a golf school junior clinic for the PGA. It was a lot of fun, too. All the kids wanted to learn and had a lot of questions for me. I headed back to Toronto to play in the Canadian Open late Wednesday night. I made the cut on Friday and played reasonably well in the Canadian Open and then I was finally able to go home to celebrate my whirlwind two weeks. It's amazing that all of this happened to me in only fourteen days!

5. *Life on the PGA TOUR*

When I married Susan the summer I graduated from Florida, I had no clue as to the tour, and everything seemed like an adventure. I still wasn't sure if I could make a living playing golf, but I was determined to try my hardest to make my dreams come true. Hilton Head was my first tournament. At that time it was out in the boondocks; it was not the built-up resort that it is today. Susan and I had little money, about eight hundred dollars between us, and it was only going to last us for a limited time. I needed a sponsor. Lucky for me John Jennings came to the rescue. He liked me, and Susan had worked for him at his bank in Florida, so he sponsored me (we later paid him back). He is still a close friend of ours to this day. On tour, one of the wives who was nicest to Susan was Bob Murphy's wife, Gail, who took Susan under her wing and showed her the ropes. Unlike in team sports such as baseball, we as golfers don't have teams making our reservations for us or giving us expense allowances. We have to be our own traveling secretaries and our own business managers.

In any case, Susan and I spent our honeymoon in Minneapolis. We only stayed in a hotel one night, then stayed with family the rest of the time. We had a new car, and little did I know that this car would be our first step as a married couple. I thought I would be playing in the Milwaukee Open, but I found out while in Chicago, where I had gone to get a lesson from Lee after our honeymoon, that I had not qualified. I had no exemption. Susan was playing tennis and I was mad that I hadn't gotten the exemption. I told her I would have to go back to Florida to play in one of those two-day tournaments down there to earn some quick paychecks. I told her, "Get in the car and go home, get our stuff in Madison and come back for me. Pick me up and we're heading to Florida." She actually just did it. She got in the car, drove all the way back by herself from Chicago to Madison and got our stuff. That's when the adventure began, or so I found out later. About halfway home the car's oil light had gone on and the car slowed down to about thirty-five mph. Susan was suddenly stuck in the middle of farm country, and there wasn't anyone around. Finally she found this farmer and went into his barn. She left him fifty cents for some oil, poured the oil into the car, and left. The light went on again. She stopped at a filling station and the attendant checked the oil and told her that the tank was one-fourth over the limit. It was full with oil. The light had gone on for other reasons. She was crying and was upset, and so he checked the car out right then for her. He noticed what had gone wrong immediately. The oil pump had fallen off during the course of the ride from Chicago. There was only one logical solution: get a new oil pump. However, although they had oil pumps they didn't know if the new one would work because the engine might have burned itself out. They tested it, and luckily it worked. If it hadn't worked Susan would have been stranded there one week, because that was how long it would have taken to get a new engine and have it installed. So she went back home, picked up our dog and all of our belongings, and came back to get me. The only problem was she got lost in the process of finding me at the golf club. Here I am, sitting there waiting for her, not knowing what she just went through and when she came to see me I greeted her in a less-than-kind manner. "Where have you been?" I asked, annoyed. This was a stupid thing to say. I should have asked her if she was okay. I made a double faux pas and I said, "Well, we've got to get moving!" Then I made the third mistake of our young marriage, and I looked inside the trunk and asked Susan in an annoyed manner where I was going to put my golf clubs. "You don't want to know," she said. She had had enough of me right then, and for good reason.

The ProAm parties at the beginning of my career were great because we got to mingle with some icons such as Lucille Ball and Neil Armstrong. Johnny Mathis sang my daughter Nichole to sleep. Mac Davis, on our trip to Morocco, played his famous "word-song" game, where he made up songs based on phrases. It was a lot of fun. I also had the fun of seeing whom I was paired with, and I actually asked Larry Gatlin what he did for a living! (Larry Gatlin still laughs about that to this day with me.) Talk about not being in the limelight or used to this life, I had no clue about this stuff. I made sure, after that, always to find out beforehand what the party guests did for a living. Howard Cosell was an interesting character, and I got to hear him speak at the ProAm dinners many a time. He was truly one of the guys that loved sports with all his heart.

There were some other fun moments on tour when the ProAms came around, because it was then that I felt like somebody. When baseball great Tommy John is happy to meet you and to play alongside you, you're in seventh heaven. Here I was in awe of these guys, and they were having fun being around me. It was a neat feeling.

In 1976, I had Susan take a 1957 Chevy from Florida, when we permanently moved back to Madison, all the way to Wisconsin without first checking out the car. As it turned out, it didn't have any decent-working windshield wipers. We had decided that we really didn't need to be in Florida just to show everyone that we were serious about golf. Moving back to Madison, Wisconsin, was great for me and for my family, and I was a lot happier back home. However, the trek back home was tough, and I had to go play golf. I went to Tucson, Arizona, and Susan and her brother and Nichole all went back to Wisconsin in that car. However, Susan found out the hard way that the windshield wipers didn't work—when the snow hit in Chicago. She also found out that there was a major detail I had forgotten to inform her of—that the car had no heating system. It was a classic! Made before built-in heaters. Forget about air conditioning, there wasn't any of that until recent years. Susan and the family made it back home in time for the Super Bowl. Speaking of football, I was a real Packer fan. It was always fun if either Green Bay was winning or Minnesota was suffering. We hated the Vikings. We were Packer fans, and still are die-hards to this day. Lambeau Field is where football should be played. I've been on the field with the guys and it's been a whole lot of fun.

The 1960s and 1970s were two decades when the tour really started to explode into the new age, but transportation was still the automobile. Young golfers like myself could not afford to jet plane over to a city, and the cities in which the golf tournaments were held were not on the major jet plane routes. Driving was the most effective, and most enjoyable, means of transportation. It was a mode that allowed you to bring your wife and kids along. The stories about things that went wrong on those trips are numerous and legendary.

I remember a locker room conversation in which one golfer was boasting how he evaded a speeding ticket. He said that when the police officer pulled alongside him he sped up and exited the road and ran to a gas station and went into the bathroom. He came out of the bathroom and thanked the officer and told him he thought he'd never make it to the bathroom on time. Richard Crawford, one of the most law-abiding and nicest guys, heard this conversation and employed this tactic when the one time he was driving with his wife and kids he saw a patrolman pull alongside him. He sped up, exited the road, and ran into a bathroom. He came out and found no officer. He had gas put into the car, went for lunch, and then pulled up the entrance ramp back onto the highway. There was the patrolman waiting on the hood of his car for him! Speeding ticket! It just goes to show you that being the nicest guy doesn't always avoid getting the ticket.

In 1978, I was playing the PGA in Oakmont in Pittsburgh. Susan was pregnant and was a week overdue with Andrea. I finished playing and on Sunday I had a reservation at Pittsburgh for a night flight. I told the courtesy car driver at the tournament that I was trying to catch a flight and I would drive the car. She told me she'd take care of everything. This woman drove like a maniac. It was like driving with Richard Petty. She drove ninety miles an hour. We got pulled over by a cop, and I told him I had to catch my flight to go home to my pregnant wife, who was a week overdue, and he said to follow him. The cop gave us an escort, and we made it to the airport. He had to write her a ticket because it had been entered in the book already, and I felt terrible because she never would have gotten that ticket if it were not for me trying to make it to the airport.

At Pinehurst one year I left early because I missed the cut. I was on I-95 heading south to Florida. The speed limit was seventy, and I was going a little over the limit, and I was pulled over by a policeman who gave me a ticket. He laughed and told me I was the fourth one that day—because of the golf tournament. Here I thought he was going to let me out of the ticket and he laughed because he had gotten me. The next year again, on I-95, at Pinehurst, I'm heading to Florida after finishing the tournament, and I was happy, and I was pulled over again by the same cop. He first tells me I'm the fourth or fifth PGA player that evening to whom he gave a ticket, then he tells me he remembers me from last year!

One year in Japan we flew to Norita. We were staying overnight at a hotel at the airport and the next morning would be leaving by bus to the tournament. We woke up, and there was plaster all over our bed. We went downstairs to check out, and everyone was downstairs milling around in a big commotion. Susan and I asked what was happening and were met by shocked looks and blank stares. One person looked at us as if we were crazy and asked, "You didn't feel the earthquake last night?" There had been an earthquake, and we'd slept through it—even though half the ceiling had fallen on our bed! It had been a 5.5 on the Richter scale. How does one sleep through that? I'm a light sleeper, which makes it all the crazier.

Traveling was fun, but the hotels never had enough cribs. At that time the hotels didn't care whether you had a family and were traveling with them. We used the dresser drawer as a crib for little Nichole. It worked out nicely. It was a pretty slick idea on our parts.

One of the things that was tough about travel were the times when you had to go to bed early and the people in the next room would have all-night parties. I would be up all night because somebody was having a blast next door, throwing chairs into the swimming pool. In that case what the older golfers told me to do was to give them a phone call when I left for the course early in the morning at about 6:00 A.M., just to see if they're awake! Oh, and diapers were fun because on airplanes you'd hold your kid in your hands before the invention of disposable diapers and you'd have these wet marks all over your pants when you arrived at your destination.

When I first started flying in the early 1970s I can remember never even making a reservation. I would drive to the airport and board a plane, and there always seemed to be one flying to every major airport. All you needed to do was just arrive at the airport and go to the counter and buy your ticket. Today you stand in line for everything, and it all adds stress to your life. Some of the worst airplane stories took place overseas in Japan. Two getaways from Japan stick out in my mind. One turned out perfect in the end, and the other was my worst nightmare at every step of the way.

I had been playing in Japan as the American representative. I had missed the cut and decided instead to help them out on Japanese television and do some commentating. I'd agreed to stay on until the last group teed-off on Saturday. We were a couple hundred miles away from Tokyo, and there was a Bullet train that left at 1:08 P.M. bound for Tokyo Station. The last group teed-off at 1:00 P.M. Once the last group hit, I had exactly eight minutes to make that train. The group took their tee swings, and I shook hands with my partners on Japanese television and said my good-byes and headed for the car the tournament director had waiting for me. They'd had my stuff already loaded. I got inside, and they drove like maniacs to get to the train station. They got me there with one minute to spare and we ran through the station with them throwing my bags into the train, stuffing me into it, and wishing me well and waving good-bye. The doors shut, and the train was bound for Tokyo. I had two hours to get to my flight. At 2:00 P.M. we arrived in Tokyo Station, and my Northwest flight from Tokyo to Chicago was scheduled to leave at 3:45 P.M. I knew I wasn't going to make it. It's an hour from Tokyo Station to Norea. Two guys from Mizzuno Golf met me at the train station. One picked up my clubs. The other picked up my suitcase. We ran through the train station, and they had a cab waiting for me. They paid the driver a ton of money and yelled instructions in Japanese. Cars in Japan have bells that go off if you speed. Well, the bells were ringing every step of the way to the airport. It was one of those deals where we made the hour trip in thirty minutes. I was scared to death. The driver was weaving in and out from the right lane to the left lane to the median at about ninety miles an hour. I had fifteen minutes before my flight was supposed to depart, and I ran to the counter hauling my luggage and gave a huge sigh that I'd made it. The ticket agent looked at me and told me he was sorry that he couldn't get me on that flight because I was not there forty-five minutes before departure. I went semi-nuts and told them I *was* getting on that flight. I had a friend in a powerful position at Northwest, and I told the agent that I would call him. He let me on that flight, all right, and I got home on time! It was one of those events that happen once in a lifetime, where everything goes as planned even though the odds are stacked against you. I still can't believe I made that flight—with my heart pounding at about 150 beats per minute.

The other story is where all goes wrong. Raymond Floyd and I were playing in Osaka. It was the U.S.–Japan matches, and we both had to leave Sunday night to get to Chicago on Monday for corporate outings. When you leave Japan you gain time because of the time zone difference. We made our presentation after the tournament and everything was perfect. We arrived at the airport and the plane was supposed to depart at seven o'clock. It was about 6:45 P.M. and there's not a heck of a lot of activity going on and we start to get nervous. We're supposed to leave in fifteen minutes. The other airplanes are leaving, and we're just sitting there. The flight attendants wouldn't give us any word on what was happening. The only reason why we were flying from Osaka to Honolulu and then from Honolulu to Chicago was because this route was the most expedient. If we knew it would have been a nightmare we'd have flown out of Tokyo. We knew something was wrong at 7:15 P.M., and we asked to leave the plane so that we could go to Tokyo. They wouldn't let us off. Now we're mad! At eight o'clock they served us dinner on the airplane and we knew that because of the noise abatement issue in the surrounding town, the airport would close at 9:00 P.M. At 8:30 P.M. the PA system came on, and we were told by a friendly voice that the plane needed a part and that we would be leaving first thing the next morning. The main problem was that we had already cleared customs and were technically not in the country. The authorities pulled a bus up to the airplane, and they took us to a hotel and had armed guards watching us round the clock. We were held hostage this night in Osaka. The next day came, and we no longer even wanted to go to Honolulu, but they made us get on that flight, which we did, and the flight finally arrived in Honolulu—just in time to miss every single connecting flight on every airline! Now Raymond and I had to spend a night in Honolulu. What should have been a trip that would have had us arriving in Chicago on Sunday night turned out to be a saga that didn't end until Tuesday morning.

Traveling on tour was not that much fun when Susan was home and I had to go alone. Golf, unlike the team sports, really can make you aware that you are by yourself, and I felt uneasy about the whole situation. I loved my wife and I loved having her around me. We were a young couple and I wanted to be with her. When Nichole was a little girl and Andrea was just born, I had to go at the whole traveling bit alone. As I said, traveling solo was not much fun, especially when it came to restaurants. Eating by myself all the time was not enjoyable to me. I had had many injuries at the time, which also made traveling not a lot of fun. Playing was hard as well.

I have always tried to balance playing the tour with family life. I never wanted golf to interfere with my having a great relationship with my daughters. Even when my daughter Nichole was at Middlebury College in Vermont, I used to drive to get her and bring her back for the summer to Wisconsin.

One of the many things that is bound to happen on tour is that a golfer is bound to have some sort of casualty on the course. Someone will often get hit by an errant golf ball during the course of a practice round. Unfortunately, in my case it was my own wife. I not only hit Susan with a golf ball during an actual round in a tournament, but I hit her three times on three different occasions. The second time I hit her accidentally with a golf ball she was standing by a tree, and I had made an errant shot. The third time I hit her by accident with a golf ball I was using my one-iron and she was by the side of the fairway. The ball went all the way down by the fairway's end and hit her on the elbow. The worst of them all was the first time she was hit by one of my golf balls. We were not even one year into our marriage; it was in

49

Chicago, 1973. It was the Western Open and I teed-off. All of a sudden I knew my shot went bad. In fact, I could see it was heading right for Susan. I started waving my hands and yelling "Fore!" to her off in the crowd. So were my paired partners. We were all waving at her in unison. All of a sudden she's waving back. I'm thinking to myself, "What is she doing waving back to me?" The next thing I knew the golf ball hit her right on the back of the head and ricocheted off her head and onto the green on a par-4 hole. It was fortunate for me, as I was able to keep the good lie on the green. More important, however, was that Susan was fine. I was still troubled, even after she told me she was feeling fine, as to why she kept waving back at me when this golf ball is flying right toward her. When I asked her about it afterward she said, "I thought it was sweet that you were waving to me." She thought it was me, her husband, waving to her out of love. Not that I wouldn't do that, but I was waving to her to get out of the way. Just another day on the links, I guess.

I remember mostly about travel that the hotels didn't even have alarm clocks, much less televisions and radios. I brought my own clock and one day it failed me, but for a good reason. I was in Pinehurst, North Carolina, and I was supposed to get up at 5:30 A.M. for my tee time. I woke up past six o'clock. Susan had set the clock for 5:30 P.M. by accident. I got out of bed, dressed quickly, ran downstairs, got in the car, raced to the golf course, and got there at 6:55. Fortunately for me there was a rain delay, which had pushed back the game one hour, and I could compete.

Another aspect of travel was the adventure of whether your luggage and/or clubs would arrive at the hotel. This happens to players all the time. One year I went to Australia to play in a tournament, and on this occasion my clubs didn't show up. I arrived on Sunday night and my clubs didn't arrive until two hours before I teed-off on Thursday. I actually thought they'd never show. I was prepared to have to make do with a set of clubs from the golf club. The baggage situation at the airports was worse before the computerized bag tags came into existence. The handwriting of the employees checking bags was so illegible that when you arrived at the baggage claim area, your bags still weren't there, but meanwhile you'd have run around from station to station for hours trying to figure out what the agent had written on your tag.

I was playing in the Bing Crosby Clambake, renamed the AT&T Classic, at Pebble Beach. All kinds of crazy things happen with clubs and luggage. For me, my clubs came and they were the only things that arrived. I had no clothes. After a few days they couldn't find my luggage. I had to buy some new clothes. I bought an entire new wardrobe, and after two weeks, when I returned from Hawaii, which was where I was heading afterward, the luggage arrived in Madison, Wisconsin. Here I am sitting at home and the luggage arrives with stamps on it from all over the world. My luggage looked like it had come out of a Bugs Bunny cartoon, with stickers on it from all different countries. Where in the world was it for two weeks? I don't even want to know the answer to that one.

Then there was Endicott, New York. A great day spoiled. I played in a tournament up there and based on my score I was pretty sure I didn't make the cut. I got into the car with Susan and we started driving to my next tournament in Ohio. We were seven hours into the trip when we stopped for dinner. It was then at dinner when I found out I was wrong. I had made the cut! I had to drive all night, seven more hours straight to get back to Endicott, and I had to play in that tournament without a minute of sleep.

One of the many neat things about playing on the PGA TOUR is that you get to be around your friends and you also get to make some new friends. Camaraderie in golf is extremely important because it's not a team sport, which makes it easy to get lonely. Practical jokes are another aspect of the goofing around that often happens among the players.

You talk about locker room camaraderie. We had a golfer by the name of George Burns who once had his shoe trees glued inside his shoes. If that's not love from one player to another, then who knows what love is really all about. . . .

Life on the tour got hard at times for me, and I guess I expressed myself through a compulsive passion for buying cars. My car stories are numerous, as at one point I owned ten or more cars, which was rather excessive. First there was the 1957 Ford Thunderbird. I had missed three cuts in a row and one of the missed cuts was the PGA Championship at Pebble Beach.

It was right before Susan made me fly to Westchester. I saw an ad in the local California paper for a 1957 Thunderbird. We went to see it, and I impulsively bought it. I drove it to Napa and left it at a friend's house, to be picked up later on after my two-day outing in Napa. I flew reluctantly to Westchester and won there, as I discussed, but the car still sat in California, and after the season was over, it needed to be retrieved. Late in the fall Susan, Nichole, and I went to Napa and got inside this tiny 1957 classic and drove it back to Madison. We had just enough room for all of our stuff, except for the trophy that I had won at Westchester. I had this great big punch bowl, and there wasn't any room for it, so Susan held it on her lap the whole way. Now you see why I picked a Cadillac that sunny summer day when my father offered me the choice of either it or a Volvo.

The idea of buying all these cars was crazy. I went through a stretch in my life where whenever I felt depressed, I bought a car. If I wasn't playing well, I went out and I bought a car. I had always admired cars as a kid. All kids want to be seen in a new car or a sports car. This car-buying obsession was a combination of a love of cars, and a rather compulsive way to take my mind off some troubling injuries and some poor playing.

Once I was out playing in a tournament in Hartford and we saw this 1966 Mustang Convertible. I played the tournament, bought the car on impulse, and drove it back to Madison. I actually did not mind driving because I had to drive anyway from tournament to tournament.

Then there was the time I even bought a car from one of my golfing comrades. I bought this Rolls-Royce from golfer Gene Littler. I bought the car, picked it up, and after playing at La Costa in California, I drove that car all the way home to Madison, Wisconsin. The only quirk was that the Rolls-Royce was not Americanized. For me, it wasn't a problem and it was a neat aspect of the car. I loved that car because it was unique for many reasons. It was a real, authentic, right-hand driven car. In fact, I was stopped for speeding in Iowa, and the policeman wanted to give Susan the ticket. He approached the car and knocked on the left side of the door and he kept asking her for her license and it took him some time before he realized that the car was a right-handed car. He was so mad because he looked foolish that he gave me the ticket. I couldn't get out of that one.

The best car story of them all was how I got my new DeLorean. I had met John DeLorean at a party at Bill Fugazy's house, and he told me that he was building this new style of car that would fit me, and so I ordered one from him. I sold the car finally because it became a hassle. This was yet another stage in my life that came to pass and which I'm glad is over. It all follows rather harmoniously with the rest of my life as I knew it on the PGA TOUR during the early 1980s, when surgeries were aplenty and my spirits were low at times. Now I just have a couple of "normal" cars in my garage.

Again, after I had won in 1978 I felt as if I were a young man without a sense of purpose. I played well in 1979 and in 1980, but because I was a father of two little girls, my number one priority was my family. My kids were important to me, and being with Susan was important to me. I became involved with the Wisconsin football team and traveled as a coach with them in the early 1980s.

Life on the PGA TOUR was terrific in 1985, however, as I won my second U.S. Open. Life continued to be great until my last days as a PGA TOUR player, with two memorable funny moments in between 1985 and the late 1990s.

In 1989, the British Open saw me with a new caddie, my friend George Gillett. George is a prominent businessman and a good friend who kept asking if he could caddie for me. The caddying experience turned the British Open into a trip, which began in Paris. We took George's jet plane to Paris and did some shopping, then headed off to Royal Lytham. I shot a 77 on Thursday, but the conditions were so tough that I knew if I could just play halfway decently the second day that I would make the cut. George's son had brought him a huge block of English toffee. On Friday, on the third hole, George broke off a slab of it and I made birdie on the hole. On the next hole George once again ate a huge hunk of that toffee and once again I made a birdie. Now I've birdied three and four. George then let his superstitions run wild and he kept eating huge slabs of this toffee and I kept making birdies. All of a sudden I'd birdied five holes in a row and he was about to go into sugar arrest. I was at the eighth hole and I was standing over my tee shot and I heard this crackling of paper. I looked back at him and he was trying to get the wrapper off a new block of toffee. I gave him a rather annoyed look and he turned around. I once again set up over the ball and he once again was crackling the paper on this block of toffee. I asked him what he was doing, and then he was embarrassed and the gallery and other players knew that I was now concentrating on my caddie for some reason and not on the shot. The guys in my group were all looking at me. He threw the hunk of toffee back into the bag. I went on to par the eighth hole, ninth hole, and the tenth hole. The birdie streak was over and rain fell on the eleventh hole. My glove was stretching itself because of all the rain, and I went

Life's great, even when I'm sitting on my golf bag.

to my bag to get a new glove. (I always have at least three gloves in my bag, just for good measure.) I pulled out a new glove and hooked to it was this big hunk of toffee, three other gloves, and a couple of balls, all stuck together. The other players in my group were laughing hysterically. I tease him about this all the time, and I was, despite my intensity, laughing when it happened.

One such moment occurred during the 1992 U.S. Open held at Pebble Beach. Cory Pavin, Jeff Sluman, Billy Andrade, and I were playing a practice round. At about the tenth hole we decided that we were going to start playing a little joke on Cory's caddie. We knew his caddie had been off for a couple of weeks, and we figured this was a good time to have some fun with both of them now that he had returned. We started putting extra stuff into Cory's bag. One of us put a rain suit in his bag. A couple of holes later someone else put their rain suit in his bag, along with golf balls, sweatshirts, and all kinds of heavy objects. At about the seventeenth hole, his caddie, "Niner," starts realizing something was wrong. He starts complaining about how he has had two weeks off and how heavy the bag felt. He said, "Gee, I've had two weeks off and I thought I'd feel more rested. This bag feels so heavy." We're all trying not to laugh. Then we got to the eighteenth hole and Niner is really complaining to Cory. He's wondering what in the world Cory has in this bag. After Cory hit his third shot, he asked Niner if he could get him his jacket. He wanted to stay warm. In the middle of the eighteenth fairway, Niner started rummaging through Cory's bag. The eighteenth fairway looked like a yard sale gone wrong. He flipped jackets and balls and everything but the kitchen sink out of that bag. The fairway was littered with all kinds of stuff. Cory just looked at all of this and then at us and we were all laughing hysterically.

6. My U.S. Open Victory at Oakland Hills

It took me a year of slumping to realize that playing with an elbow that didn't work at all wasn't the right decision. For two and a half years prior to 1985 I was not too much of a player, and the articles about my not deserving to win the first U.S. Open really wore on my family and friends.

During 1983 I was swinging to compensate for the pain shooting down my entire arm. At the end of the year, I decided it was time for an operation on my elbow. After the operation, in 1984, I made a lot of cuts but finished at the bottom every single week. I spent most of the year relearning my golf swing and getting ready for the next year. I had a lot of unlearning to do, after developing the wrong type of muscle memory by playing hurt that year. In retrospect, I should have stopped playing and had the operation immediately. I knew at the end of the '84 golf season, however, that I was getting closer. During the winter of 1984, I worked hard in the off season with respect to conditioning and rehabilitating my arm. I practiced so much I thought I'd go crazy.

When 1985 started off, things felt like they were ready to click for me. I had a good tournament at the Hawaiian Open to start things off, and I felt like I could play again. I played well that spring, finishing in the top 10 more than once. This was the first event in which I played well, finishing sixth. I finished fourth at the Western Open. I missed the cut at Westchester the week before the U.S. Open, but I did not take this as a sign of bad luck.

I flew out to Oakland Hills with some confidence. I registered and practiced on Sunday, the week before, and I felt as if I had found something in my swing that worked for me out on that practice tee. I had some more great practice rounds on Monday and Tuesday of that U.S. Open week. I played so well during Wednesday's practice round, I knew I was ready for something special. After nine holes things felt great, and I relaxed and saw a movie.

I was reading the U.S. Open program and I noticed that Ralph Guldahl had won two U.S. Opens: Cherry Hills and Oakland Hills. It got me thinking about winning and doing the same.

I was paired with David Graham and Johnny Miller for the first two rounds. On Thursday, round one, I shot a 70, par for the U.S. Open, so I was in good shape for Friday. It was certainly good enough to get me in the thick of things.

I went out and shot 65 on Friday. I played really well and was a couple of strokes back off the lead. I was in the top 5 for sure. I honestly don't think I could have played better. As we signed our scorecards at the end of the round Friday, Johnny Miller told me that I was playing so well he knew I was going to win the whole thing.

On Saturday the front that the meteorologists had predicted all week long finally came through, and it was windy, cold, and rainy. I looked like a drowned rat in the photos that day. I had my rain suit on, then decided to take it off after the first few holes because it was affecting my game. However, I shot well enough—a 70—this day to win. Saturday, to me, was the day I won the U.S. Open. It separated me from all the rest. T. C. Chen was leading, and I was in second place. The rest of the guys shot 73 or 74 and fell off the leaderboard. I was inside the press room and one of the writers stood up and said,

"Since it was a fluke that you won in 1978, do you think you have any chance of winning this year?" I now wanted to prove him and the rest of the media wrong about me, that I was not a fluke.

Sunday didn't start so well for me: a bogey on the first and then only a par on the second, a hole I should have birdied. T. C. Chen, meanwhile, birdied both, and I went from just one stroke behind to four shots back in only two holes. He was playing beautifully until he made his famous double hit at the par-4 fifth hole. It all started on his second shot, when, instead of putting the ball in the middle of the green, since the hole was a tough pin placed at the right side of the green, he played an aggressive shot at the pin and hit it way right. Then he tried to hit a pitch shot and bounce it through the rough, which didn't work. This left him with his fourth shot. He was in the deep rough and the ball unfortunately came out so that the club hit the ball twice on the same swing. He made an 8 on that hole, and I made a 4. Suddenly we were tied for the lead.

Things were clicking for me again. I had the joy of being the co-leader going into the ninth hole, and I went ahead and bogeyed holes 9 and 10, and 11! Can you believe that? Now things are slipping away. We had let everyone else back into the game. I was upset with my play to say the least. I didn't have that many good shots, and I was in a mess.

I had driven the ball into the fairway bunker, and so I hit a five-iron. The swing felt terrific. The shot was a round changer for me. The ball landed right down the heart of the fairway. I ended up missing an eight-foot putt for birdie, but I was confident going into the thirteenth hole because my swing was under control. I knew the bogey streak had ended. I had made my par at the terrible twelfth hole.

The thirteenth hole was also kind to me. The hole is a great par-3 that played about 185 yards to the green. I took out my five-iron and hit a great tee shot that landed within fifteen feet of the hole. I made that birdie putt and I was sort of back in control. It tied me for the lead. I shot par over the next three holes, which were hard par-4 holes. As I approached hole 17 I was still tied for the lead. I promptly hit a ball into the greenside bunker on this hard par-3 hole. However, I did save par here, and I managed to gain the lead going to hole 18.

What made the seventeenth hole so difficult was there was a ridge of about six feet high in the middle of the green, which cut the green in half. The pin was on the right side of the mound, and the ball was on the left side. You could not two-putt from one side of the mound to the other. It just couldn't be done. I had spent a lot of practice rounds on that green studying it, and I knew that I had to be on the right half of the green to have any chance to get it on the right. I came up short of the hole, and my ball landed in the bunker. The bunker was a much easier shot, however, than if my ball had landed on the left side of the green. I ended up almost making the bunker shot for a birdie but missed by two inches and tapped in for a great par.

I strolled to the eighteenth hole now in a great frame of mind. The eighteenth hole was a par-5 for the members but, as at Cherry Hills, a par-4 for us. Its dog-leg right was extremely tough to play. To top it all off there was a nice, deep, bunker on the right, and some deep bunkers on the left of the fairway. Even after a perfect tee shot, you still have a four- or five-iron to make it to the green, and that's if you can hit long. The eighteenth hole at Oakland Hills forces you to play short of the green, as opposed to being long. If you are over the green here, you're dead. Once you're on the green you'll thank your lucky stars you made it there. But I had confidence, and my tee shot was perfect. My second shot, no matter what, was going to be either a four- or a five-iron. The group in front of me made bogey, and I knew now that I also could make a 5 on this hole and still win the U.S. Open. With my two-shot lead now firmly in hand, I took my second stroke and I made it a great one. I landed the ball just short of the green, to set up an easy pitch. I pitched up just ten feet short of the hole and was now ready for a two-putt situation. The green on the eighteenth hole at Oakland Hills is

The State of Wisconsin declared "Andy North Day" when I won the second U.S. Open in 1985. Andrea, Nichole, Susan, and I celebrated.

severely sloped from back to front. I wanted to make sure that I kept the ball at the lowest end of the hole. I two-putted and won the Open and silenced my critics.

This win came at a time when I did not expect to win. In 1978 I had expected to win a major because I was young and starting out and felt healthy. At this time in my career I had played well during the spring, but I was not at that stage where I thought I could win a major given my recent surgery and injury. Half of the bogeys for the week I made in the last day. I went inside the press room and felt that nobody would now say I was a lucky player. A lot was made of T. C. Chen's shot, but I performed when I had to and I won it all.

I had played well all week except on Sunday, but I won and I did it in front of my parents, who were in the stands. It was Father's Day and my mom and dad saw me win my second U.S. Open in person. Unfortunately Susan and the kids weren't there to see me win, once again. She was going to fly over and watch me on Sunday, but she decided she didn't want to make me nervous, and that was pretty big of her to think that way. Winning was special because it made me feel as if I had the best years ahead of me.

The rest of 1985 was good to me. I played well and had some great rounds and I made the prestigious Ryder Cup team. I was so excited about making this team, and it meant everything to me. Needless to say, when I didn't play well for the team I was devastated. There is nothing like standing up at the opening ceremonies and having them play the national anthem and getting all choked up. I'll never forget what it felt like to represent my country; it was the greatest feeling, and the most disappointing thing I've ever gone through in all of my years in athletics.

7. My Golfing Career

Growing up in Madison, Wisconsin, yet another side story, is a rather important part of my golfing career. There is a quality of life here that is fantastic. There are many parks and great golf courses, and the schools are great. Crime is low and values are intact. These aspects have affected me in more ways than one might think. Because I grew up in the Midwest I always persevered through my injuries because I had that hard-life and tough-spirit mentality.

I always believed something good was going to happen and that it was right around the corner. I had no clue about drugs growing up, and so when I had the good life it did not go to my head and make me want to party until I was nuts. I had my feet on the ground because I lived in Madison during the formative phases of life, and it has everything to do with what I'm about today. Madison gave me a "Welcome Home, Andy North Day." It's such a comfortable place to come home to because the whole city is built and centered around four distinct lakes. This makes not only for some breathtaking scenery but also for the ability to partake in water sports. There are a ton of outdoor activities to do, such as ice skating, skiing, and climbing. This outdoors mentality led me to think a certain way. Madison has been home to me and will always be home to me. I feel it's because of the values that were instilled in me during my childhood, this Midwest mentality, that are a part of my being and my ability to never fear that I'm down and out, even when things haven't gone my way.

There are two possible manners in which to view my career: either I was very disappointing or I won two U.S. Opens and did the best I could despite serious injuries. I think the biggest aspect to my career is that I lived my dream. I had an awful lot of fun doing what I've done and I've lived well.

Over the course of my career I have had six knee operations, a toe operation, a neck operation, a thumb operation, and an elbow operation, and I even joked about it with Jim Taylor of the Green Bay Packers. Jim and I were sitting around at the dinner table at a Special Olympics event, and he said he had never had one operation. Imagine playing the rough and tumble game of football and never needing an operation? This was back in the days of little or no padding, which makes it even more astonishing. In fact, my wife is such a Packer fan that she bid for the Special Olympics auction on an autographed Jim Taylor football and outbid everyone. He came over to me later and said, "Andy, if I had known Susan wanted the ball that badly, I'd have given it to her." Now he tells me, after Susan spent all the money— and it cost a pretty penny. It was worth it, though, because it was all for charity, and the Special Olympics is one charity that Susan and I have been privileged to have been associated with over the years. The real question everyone always asks me is when all of the injuries started for me and whether I feel disappointed in my PGA performance.

The injuries, and operations, began for me in 1970 in college. I had my first of many knee operations. I hurt my knee playing a pickup basketball game. I had finished fourth in the NCAA that year and went in for surgery after classes finished at the beginning of the summer. Back then there weren't any scopes or ten-day recovery plans. I had the full-fledged eight- or ten-inch scar and lay in bed the whole summer. The first round of golf I played that summer was for the National Amateur, and I ended up being able to qualify, after what I call slapping the ball around. In the fall of 1983, I had a bone spur removed from my elbow. It ruined the rest of the year and all of 1984.

In 1984, I had to relearn to swing. I'm often asked what it was like to go through my many surgeries. I was at a point where I thought my thirties would be filled with more U.S. Opens and other major victories, but things didn't pan out that way. Having a surgery didn't bother me. What was tough was the rehabilitation afterward. It required me to spend all of my time concentrating on rehab and not on golf. It seemed as if for fifteen years all I did was rehab. I would play a few tournaments at the start of the year, and then I would have to have surgery and rehab for the rest of the year. All of a sudden I'm thirty-two and there's another year of my golfing life gone in the blink of an eye. Nevertheless, I wouldn't trade what's happened to me for anything. I've had a great time of it, and I've always loved this game and my life, but sometimes I wondered what it would have been like to not have been plagued by constant injuries. It would have been fun to see what I could have done if I had been healthier, especially since I won my first U.S. Open in my twenties.

What was rehab like? What did it consist of? Rehabilitation was different for me for different injuries, but the one aspect common to all of the injuries was that I would go months before I was allowed, after surgery, to touch a golf club. My doctors were very aggressive in working on my knees, and within an hour of an operation I was on the exercise bicycle. The hours of physical therapy and weight lifting needed to be put in to make the whole thing work. The idea of not being able to pick up a golf club centered around the general philosophy my doctors had about operations. They felt my legs needed to be strong before I could place all that stress again on my knees. I was told that if I rushed rehab I would compensate by putting undue pressure on my other knee, and then I would have problems with that knee. It was important to swim and get the flexibility back in my knee before I started swinging golf clubs. Most people don't rehabilitate themselves properly after an operation. They end up straining other parts of their body to compensate for the weakness in the area of their body on which they were operated.

I always went through my routine properly, and I always felt like these operations were just a bump in the road and were no big deal. What I looked forward to was the idea of feeling better after all this was done. There is nothing better than having the pain eased in your body. That's when you feel good about things in your life. As I lived these injuries, I always felt that tomorrow would be better. You're going one day at a time or one week at a time. The process of rehabilitation from day to day allows one to see changes and improvement, and the frustrating part is when you go two or three days and you don't feel any improvement. That has happened to me on occasions, and I've told myself that rehab is a lot like watching kids grow up. You don't see any change from day to day, and then all of a sudden they're big kids. If you were to not see them for a month, then you would notice the change in their growth. You'd say to yourself, "Oh my God, they've gotten so big!" It's the same with rehab. After a while your injuries do heal, but the real test is at the practice range a year later.

Hitting golf balls that first time after rehabilitation was always the hardest part of the whole ordeal. The reason was that I knew how it felt to play healthy and I knew how to play with an injury, but picking up that golf club after a year and not having felt it is a scary feeling. I have often wondered whether I would ever get that feeling back at all in my life. Sometimes your golf swing is so messed up that it never comes back to you. It has happened to some players. They get an injury and they're never the same. The most difficult aspect to hitting after an incredible layoff is hoping to find that muscle memory and feeling. I've always been a strong believer my whole life that if you're working diligently, you'll get better. I've always felt that there would

Susan and me at the 1985 Ryder Cup

be a reward in the end. This was my way of dealing with things. Life on the PGA tour is all about the ups and downs, because life in general is about ups and downs.

In 1986, I started off well but broke my hand in March. I fell down and tried to catch myself but ended up breaking my right hand, which forced me to spend eight weeks in a cast. During rehabilitation I strengthened my right hand so much that it was too strong for my left hand. This was the start of my body giving up. My body didn't work very well. I had five knee operations between 1986 and 1992. I had my neck operated on in 1989 because of bone spurs, which started from a car accident in senior year in high school when our car rolled over two or three times. I couldn't play at all, and at some point in time I had some years in the early 1990s that terrified me, such as when I had skin cancer. Unlike a regular operation, in which bones are fixed or skin removed, this operation centered around removing tissue from my nose, where they carved and carved until a large amount of basal cell was removed. I needed plastic surgery afterward to reconstruct my nose.

The waiting game was terrible with regard to my skin cancer. The way it worked was as follows: I would have an operation to remove cancerous cells from my nose, and each time I needed to follow up with a phone call to find out if all was well. Each time the surgeons told me that they needed to remove more tissue. This repeated itself four times! I don't know if I could have withstood another operation because it was at the point where the doctors said on the fourth time that they had removed everything possible. They also told me that there wasn't much more room for error because my nose would not be able to withstand more surgeries. The summer days as a kid spent sunning myself and in college at the University of Florida had taken their toll on me. I was now more conscious about the sun and skin cancer.

The other operations, aside from the neck operation, were all local-anesthetic operations, for which I was awake and alert. The nose operations to remove skin cancer were deep-anesthesia operations and were dangerous. I did the best I could in each situation, and sometimes I could not silence my critics. I just said that given all my injuries the best I could do on a specific day in 1994 was 73 or 74. I was at my wit's end. I tried hard all the time, and I had to come to grips with the fact that after 1985 my PGA career was waning, even though I was only in my thirties. It was tough to go to the golf course and know I had no chance of competing with the other guys. There were some days I wondered why I was even doing this; probably because I was bold-headed and stubborn. The natural inclination of an athlete is never to give up. Sometimes it worked and sometimes it surely didn't. But my waning career led me to get interested in television and ESPN.

Broadcasting gave my body a chance to heal, I returned to actively playing golf in 2000, when I turned fifty, and could play on the SENIOR PGA TOUR.

Although I had a career shortened by surgeries in the early years, I feel better today at age fifty-one than I did early in my career, and it's a great relief not to have to see an operating room.

Part Two

Improving Your Golf Game

*Improvement comes with a little instruction,
a lot more practice, and a whole lot of love
for the game.*

8. Good Foundations

THE GRIP

One of the best ways to improve your long game is to have a great foundation. Too many people get far too concerned with the hundred and fifty different things they read in books or magazines about how to improve their game. If most people would start with a proper club grip, then their entire game would be better.

My secret of success was finding my natural grip, which happened during high school when I met Manuel de la Torre. The day I broke his beautiful shag bag was the day I knew how the club felt when I made contact with an object using the correct swing.

I firmly believe that very few average players ever grip the golf club properly, so finding the proper grip is almost impossible! Most golfers who have an incorrect grip will never be able to lower their score, no matter how hard they try, until they change their grip. Either listen to my advice, or don't complain.

The club, for a right-handed golfer, should be held in the last three fingers of the left hand, where the pressure is, up against the little pad in your left palm. There's a V created between your thumb and forefinger in your left hand, so it points at the right side of your head. The valley of the palm of your right hand fits right over the thumb in the left hand. Then the V in your right hand points in the same direction over the V in your left hand. The pressure is in the left hand, and the right hand is really lightly gripped around the club.

If everybody could have a good grip and if everybody could get set up over the ball with the ball in the right position in the stance and aimed in the right direction, then everyone would improve dramatically without working on the actual golf swing. This would lead to better play.

JUNIOR GOLF

Parents come over to me and ask me all the time when to start giving their children lessons and my answer is always the same. I tell them that when their child is old enough to understand the game and the etiquette of the game, and the child wants to be with the parent, then it's time to take them along on the course. They will learn skills that are good for life in general. The game is not as expensive as everyone thinks it is. Little kids like to go to the driving ranges and just pound golf balls. I was lucky to have had people like my dad who cared for me. He gave me the equipment and the time necessary to play the game of golf.

The key to my swing has been to swing all the clubs in my bag the same way. The driver, to me, was no different a club than an iron with respect to my swing. I swing my driver the same way I swing my six-iron, to this very day. I don't agree with people who say the swing should be different. Find your swing and repeat it for each club, as opposed to having fourteen different swings. Different swings just compound any problems already inherent in your golf swing.

Junior golf is important to the game of golf. Junior golf is the reason why the game of golf continues to grow. Most of the golfers reading this book will be teaching their kids to play golf, and the kids should learn to love the game and to have fun playing it. How many games can a child play at the age of five and continue to play their whole life? This is the only game where grandparents can play *with* their grandchildren, instead of just watching them. It can't be done in basketball, baseball, tennis, or football.

From a competition standpoint, golf is the only game of its kind because players of all levels can play together. It's not the same in any other sports. Play one-on-one against Michael Jordan or Shaquille O'Neal and they will destroy you every time without your even getting a point ever from either of them. In golf, on any given hole you as an amateur can beat a professional. You just won't do it very often or else you'd be on tour. Even in tennis the situation is not like golf. If you're a scratch tennis player and you're playing a twenty-handicapped tennis player, then the game will be over without that less-capable player scoring a point. It's not much fun for either player. In golf, the handicapping system makes the game enjoyable for all.

COURSE MANAGEMENT

As for golf course management, there's no one perfect way to play a golf hole. Let's say you have a 380-yard par-4 hole on a course and on that hole there is a bunker at 200 yards and another bunker at 250 yards, then there are three distinctly different ways to approach that hole.

For instance, you can lay up short of the first bunker and play a 190-yard first shot, then have a 190-yard second shot to make it onto the green in two shots, giving yourself a birdie opportunity.

The second way to approach this hole is to play a shot that carries over the first bunker and falls short of the second bunker. In this way your drive is 225 yards and you're left with a 155-yard shot to get onto the green in two shots.

The third option is to take both bunkers out of play and hit a shot 280 yards and leave yourself with a wedge shot of 100 yards and a possible eagle or a birdie opportunity.

Depending on your own game, one of these methods will be guaranteed to work for you. However, you must be honest with me and with yourself. If you know you're not a 280-yard hitter, then don't try my third option. *Honesty* is the key to golf, both in scoring and in playing well!

Course management is a product of strategy when you approach the tee and being honest with yourself. Most people just go up to the tee and then strike the ball as hard as possible with their driver. They end up in a bunker or in a bad position, and they wonder why this happens to them. It happens because they don't plan ahead and they won't let themselves be honest with their own game. If they know they can hit a five-wood better than a driver, then use the five-wood and make that ball go 190 yards. My way of playing the hole would be to try and knock it over all of the bunkers, but that's only because I know I can drive the ball 280 yards.

Just remember, it's the final score on the hole that counts. Is the ego of using the driver worth the gamble of messing up the hole? Trust me, it's not worth it. Many times I myself will be on a par-5 hole with a lake in front of me and I will lay up, as opposed to going for the green immediately and possibly knocking the ball into the water.

Often the amateur doesn't understand the difference between playing a bad shot from a physical and mechanical standpoint as opposed to playing a hole poorly from a mental standpoint.

Most players who shoot in the hundreds can probably take ten strokes off their golf game if they would improve their course management. The thinking golfer will always beat the guy who goes out onto the golf course to pound balls.

When I ask most players how they shot 100 they can't tell me. Their scorecard is right in front of them and they don't know what happened to them. To fix your game, you have to be able to analyze it and to understand what went wrong. A perfect example: You add up your putts at the end of your round and they total 36. How do you know whether you've putted well or not?

If your first putt was sixty feet from the cup on every hole, then averaging two putts per hole would be terrific. However, if your first putt was ten feet from the hole, you've putted poorly averaging two putts per hole.

This begs the question of what to practice, and how to practice at the local driving range.

WHAT TO PRACTICE AND HOW TO PRACTICE

Going to the practice range is important. First, you need to stretch out your body. This sounds rather simplistic, but it's a very important aspect of practicing that often gets neglected. If you are not stretched out, you won't be able to hit the ball to your full potential and you might pull a muscle.

Second, I always place a club on the ground lying with its face side up. I use that club as my "guide," so that when I take my swing, I am able to make sure that it is always level and straight. At the same time, I also want to make sure that my body is always pointed in the direction in which I want to hit the ball. Your hips, shoulders, and feet should be square to that club line on the ground. I sometimes place a second club on the ground perpendicular to this club so that I can gauge the placement of the ball. If I wanted the ball to be in the middle of my stance, then that perpendicular club would be placed in the middle of the stance. This technique of laying a club on the ground as a guide works well because it removes other obstacles from your mind so that you can concentrate on your swing and your ball-striking technique.

The one aspect of a golfer's game that gets neglected at the practice range is the short game, and the wedge shots in particular. Your wedges are the most important clubs to use at the driving range because they teach you not to swing so hard. By not swinging hard, you train your body to hit the ball straighter and to keep yourself within proper rhythm and tempo at all times.

Another piece of advice of mine is to hit balls using all your clubs at the driving range so as to eliminate relying on a particular club. You want to be loose when you use that driver or three-wood, and the only way to keep your body loose is to practice with the shorter, more lofty, clubs first. This way you have your best chance to hit a good shot when you take out your five-wood, or three-wood.

Let's say I hit fifty or sixty shots using my short irons. I then might only hit twenty or twenty-five shots with my long irons. I might also only hit twenty-five shots with my woods, just so that my swing doesn't accelerate to a point where I've lost my rhythm. You need to be able to use any club at any time, and you need to be able to bring back the particular muscle memory for that club.

There are times when a player is swinging too hard at the practice range. This has happened to me sometimes. When this happens, I usually take out my seven-iron and hit with that club to regain my rhythm, and once my rhythm is recovered, I will then only hit one or two balls with my driver. The seven-iron is a middle iron that is neither a long iron or a short iron. It is the perfect club in length and club-head loft to help you regain your tempo and composure.

Most people in general swing their clubs too hard. This happens because they are always using the driver at the range. My advice is to use the shorter irons in your bag at the driving range until you have established a good rhythm and then use your driver and three- or five-wood clubs. Most of all, know when to quit.

The law of diminishing returns also applies. There are times when a person is tired, and after hitting twenty balls a person might be tired. Each person must know their limitations. There is no one thing everybody can do to get better.

There's no one right way to find your swing, and when you lose your swing there is no one perfect way to regain it. Sometimes the best medicine is stepping away from the game and taking some time off from golf. Sometimes I've walked away from the game for a few days.

It's more what's inside a person's head than what's "inside" their muscles. I tell people it's not the swing but the brain that's plaguing them. Jack Nicklaus had so many events happening in his life because of his stature in golf that these distractions actually helped him because they took his mind off his game when he needed a rest.

In 1981, I started my year off horrifically. I was pitiful. I had only made around three thousand dollars up until the midway point of the season. I couldn't do anything right, and yet I was practicing all the time. My mind was playing tricks on me, and I kept thinking about my swing while on the golf course and in the PGA events. It just made matters worse for me. I finally decided, when I finished at Muirfield, to just warm up before a round, and I stopped practicing and thinking mechanics and my season turned out well. I finished second place twice and ended up in the top 40 on the money list that year. It just goes to show you that sometimes thinking too hard can be lethal on the golf course.

The biggest mistake most people make in using their long irons is that they try and help lift the ball up into the air with the club. Usually what happens is that the opposite occurs. They end up staying behind the ball and topping it because the center of their golf swing has moved from over the ball to behind the ball. When this occurs one of two things happens: either the golfer hits the ball "fat" or they "top" the ball. The hardest aspect to the long-iron game is to keep the swing the same as if you were using a nine-iron or an eight-iron. There is plenty of loft to the club face so that you don't need to help your club with your body. That is built into the design of the club.

Ball placement is important in all phases of the game, but especially in the long game. For the right-handed golfer, the ball should be situated off your left foot when you are using your driver, more toward the middle but still a bit left when using the long irons, and in the center of your stance when using the short irons.

LOWERING YOUR SCORE

Keep in mind, however, that it's far easier for the amateur golfer to go from 100 to 80 than it is for the amateur to lower their score from 80 to 70. There's the old story of the twin brothers. Both play a hundred rounds of golf per year. One brother is conservative and plays smart. The other brother plays dumb and is so aggressive that he never met a lake he didn't try to hit over. The aggressive brother will have the twenty best rounds of the year. However, he'll have the thirty or forty worst rounds. The smart brother will play more consistently and will be able to lower his golf score a lot quicker. On a perfect day, the dummy wins. On a normal day, the smart one wins.

PRE-SHOT ROUTINE

What should people be thinking when they address the ball at the first tee? I think a pre-shot routine is very important. It makes responding under pressure much easier. However, the pre-shot routine does not have to take, and should not take, forty-five seconds. It should be something simple, where you get over the ball, look up at your target, waggle the club, and then go from there and begin to "play" golf. The longer you stand over your shots, the worse your position for most amateurs. You get tight, you think too much, and you think in all directions. So you're not only preoccupied at this point, but you're more than likely preoccupied to such a degree that there's no going back. Have a routine that's as fluid and fast as possible. As far as things that go through our heads during our full swing, we are all guilty of thinking too much at times.

THE PROPER SETUP

In the cases of most weekend golfers, I find that if I can get them to have a good setup with regard to ball position and alignment, then great things follow. For instance, if I start them off with a good setup and their ball alignment is perfect, then it is far easier for them to keep their body within balance and to develop a rhythm in their swing. Once the rhythm in the swing becomes an automatic part of the muscle memory, then they'll be in great shape for the entire game. The tee shot will be a good one, and they will be relaxed and have a great hole. If they start off with a great hole, it will lead to seventeen other great holes. Even if they stumble in between on holes or their ball gets trapped in bunkers, they will have the mind-set and the muscle memory to re-find their swing and recover nicely.

However, we always impose problems on ourselves, never really allowing ourselves to be happy with who we are as golfers, or with our limitations. Distance is one such problem that is plaguing everyone. The idea of pounding the ball 300 yards is a golfer's dream. People are always trying to impress someone by driving that ball 300 yards, and it usually goes off the fairway and into trouble.

THE DISTANCE FACTOR

The one critical aspect of distance is that distance is really a function of everything working together properly. The grip, the arms and shoulders, the weight shift, the twisting of your body must all be in harmony to generate the club-head speed necessary to in turn translate into distance. One of the great SENIOR PGA TOUR events is the NFL Cadillac Classic. This is an event that teams NFL greats with Senior PGA players. Al Del Grecco is a great golfer. Vinny Testaverde loves the game of golf. These athletes love golf and they are, by far, the biggest of the athletes. Its almost funny to see the Senior PGA players arrive on the tee and stand alongside these strong hulking pro football players. Yet, when each guy swings the club it's evident who the long guys are and who are the not-so-good players. The Seniors, who weigh one-half of what the NFL players weigh and are twice the age at sixty years old, hit longer and straighter than the NFL linemen in their early thirties. Even the NFL guys want to know why they can't hit the ball as far as the professional golfers and, more important, why they don't hit the ball straight. My answer is simple. It's all happening because they cannot time their motion properly. They're sometimes too strong for their own good.

Let's take an Olympic sport as an example to further illustrate an important point. Look at how throwing the shot-put has changed. For years and years the shot-put athletes would bend down and sling it up into the air. Now, the shot-put resembles the discus. The speed created with this new throwing motion generates more power. It allows the shot-putter to be longer.

The same principle can be applied to the game of golf. The speed created by turning the trunk of your body helps achieve greater distance. It has nothing to do with strength as much as it does speed. You can see this principle in action when you look at a player like Tiger Woods, who creates so much speed because he is able to turn the trunk of his body so much. When he releases it, he is able to generate speed because he's coiled up so much that it uncoils him. Tom Watson could also always create a huge amount of speed with his body.

There have been quite a few golfers shorter in stature who are great long hitters. Chi Chi Rodriguez has been a great long hitter for many years. One of the longer hitters in golf, pound for pound, is Jeff Sluman. Jeff Sluman is five seven and 145 pounds and yet he averages in the 280s in driving yardage. As I've already said, if you were to get some big linemen in football, who are some of the strongest individuals around, many cannot hit the ball far at all. Yet, there's that seventy-year-old who weighs 175 pounds and he hits the ball 250 yards. It's all about motion of the body and speed.

CLUB SELECTION

When do I hit an iron and when do I hit a wood off the fairway.

Oftentimes, a player will be better served by using a four- or five-wood or even a seven-wood than by using a long iron. The new generation of clubs, especially the Calloway Clubs that I use, allow for the amateur, as well as the professional golfer, to have more control over the golf ball. The heads of the irons and woods are designed to help the golfer put the ball up into the air easier. If I'm on a par-5 hole, which I know I can't reach in two shots, sometimes I will use the iron instead of the three-wood so that I can put myself in excellent position for a great third shot, as opposed to blasting away with a three-wood. I'd rather have that eighty-yard shot left as my third shot than possibly miss the green using the three-wood and end up in the rough for a horrific third shot. If I'm 240 yards away from the hole, I won't use the iron. I will use the three-wood at that point. Again, the situation dictates the club selection.

SHOULD THE LEFT ARM BE KEPT STRAIGHT?

Keeping the left arm straight has been a cardinal rule. Is it important? Not *all* PGA tour players keep their left arm straight! The beauty of this game we call golf is that there are a million different ways to play it, not just one way as taught by some teaching professional and a textbook. Jim Furyk has a unique swing and he plays exceptionally well with it. People are too concerned with "the perfect way." Gibby Gilbert won many times on the PGA TOUR and SENIOR PGA TOUR and he bends his left arm twenty or thirty degrees. Calvin Peete hurt his arm as a young man and he could never straighten it, and he had a great golfing career—so there goes the "keep your left arm straight" out the window. There are some basic things we all try to do in this game, but it doesn't necessarily mean you're going to be a better player if you do those things. Quite often the guys with funny swings do very, very well and then they try to improve their swing and "look better." Sometimes the swing that might make some teaching professional tell a student not to take up golf is the right swing for that person and they could be a great golfer on the PGA TOUR some day with that brutal-looking swing.

THE YARDAGE FACTOR

The players and caddies have those big discussions about the yardage from the fairway to the front of the green. I think the biggest rewards and returns for the amateur golfer to improve his or her game is to find that special place where they can go to hit shots and then pace off how far the average balls traveled. In other words, take a nine-iron out of your bag. Hit fifty balls with that nine-iron from a given point. Then pace off the yardage to the middle of the pile of nine-irons. If your nine-iron shot goes 120 yards on average, then you know when you're on the golf course you need your nine-iron for a 120-yard shot, even if the person next to you is using his or her sand wedge.

PRACTICE DEVICES

This is why there are so many devices that force the golfer to grip the club correctly, even though it doesn't feel "natural" for them. The bottom line question is, "Do these products work?" The answer is yes. However, can you use them on tour? No. So why bother to buy them? You need to develop the right swing, and that comes again from practice and muscle memory. Some of these devices are good because they help you, and force you, to have the right grip and the right arm and shoulder motions, and consequently the right swing. As you repeat the process again and again, your muscles develop a muscle memory.

I've done some infomercials for some great products. One product is called the Tempo Trainer and the other product is called the Angle Iron. Both are practice devices to help you learn how to swing better. The trouble with most of that stuff is that people don't want to have to work hard to get better. Most people want to buy a new driver that saves them ten shots, or a wedge that saves them ten shots, or the newest putter that will save their short game on the green. Most practice devices don't do well because people have to actually practice with them.

The Tempo Trainer works like magic. (I did the commercial with Lee Trevino.) It is a little device which is placed on the ground next to your ball. You have this reflector on the golf club, and when you take your backswing and follow through it will give you the elapsed time of your swing and the speed of the club head at impact. What is proved is that the slower the club is swung, in terms of overall time, the more club-head speed is created. I thought this product was going to be the greatest thing in the world. The informercials were great. However, almost no one bought the product because they'd have to go out and practice. If the commercial had us saying, "Buy this driver and hit the ball forty yards longer," the product would have sold millions. It's amazing how many people buy into this line of thinking, and that's why there are so many drivers being sold that don't add one yard of distance to your game. People want to buy something that automatically makes them a better player.

9. Golf Games That Teach

Lee Milligan taught me during my formative years in golf, and he gave me an invaluable appreciation of all facets of the game of golf. Lee and I played a game on the tee in which he made me hit three balls: a cut shot, a straight shot, and a hook shot. To be able to position your body so as to fade or slice off the tee, and not sacrifice accuracy in the process, is quite a feat. However, all three shots are important to a golfer's repertoire and should be practiced by kids. It's hard to teach adults new tricks but easy to teach children, and the future of golf lies in kids who are eight, nine, and ten years old today.

CALL-A-SHOT

At an early age Lee was teaching me about curvature of flight and control of the ball. Many times players don't think about the shot ahead of them, and they should be thinking about it. Lee was the first person to introduce me to the call-a-shot game. The game worked as follows: He might tee-off and the ball might land on the fairway, and then he would tell me, or he would call, my next shot. He might have me hit a high, soft four-iron, or a hard seven-iron, where you try to hit different kinds of shots to achieve the same result. Instead of hitting a wedge shot from ninety yards and having it just flop onto the green,

Lee would have me play a bump and run. He would have me purposely strike the ball so as to have it bounce on the fringe of the green and then roll fluidly onto the green. These drills made me think about the game of golf rather than just play the game of golf. This was what was most important about Lee's drills. Lee spoke to me at length about rhythm and balance, and his drills beautifully illustrated the importance of being in balance and in rhythm.

Sometimes you never know your creative limits until you try your hand at something novel, even if it involves something you're already used to doing. I played one of the most interesting rounds of golf in my life when I was already on the PGA tour and for a completely different reason than golf. Here I was a professional golfer and a champion and yet I never knew that the things my friends did that day could be done with a golf club. As a kid you always think of the extremes in everything you do, such as playing tennis left-handed if you're a right-handed tennis player. You might dream what it would be like to take free throws in basketball with your other hand or to switch-pitch in baseball. This happened on the golf course, but as an adult with me and some of my friends on the tour.

It was a sunny day and I was practicing with Tom Watson, John Mahaffey, and Hubert Green during the practice round of one of the tournaments in which we were playing. We had played the first nine holes and then were bored out of our minds. We needed to do something to loosen us up and then the thought came to us. On the back nine holes we decided to play call-a-shot.

For instance, I might have the tee shot on the tenth hole, and I would "call" it that everyone has to hit a seventy-five yard hook shot over a bunch of trees and land the ball right onto the fairway. Then Tom, Hubert, and John would have to, one by one, attempt making that particular shot. They all did it, and the results were hilarious. That was just the first shot on the hole. Then the second shot might be Hubert's shot, and he would "call" that everyone has to hit a forty-yard shot using a three-iron onto the heart of the green, from no matter where that first crazy shot took you that I had conceived of off the tee. In other words, you were always adding upon someone else's crazy idea. It was the insane built upon the insane.

At the end of the day we had a following. We actually had a little gallery of people who were curious as to what we were doing. There were people following us because of the crazy shots we were attempting. These were shots you'd dream about and as children dare your friends to do but would never, ever attempt to try them during a PGA tournament. We were trying shots nobody would ever attempt in their wildest dreams.

My hat's off to Hubert, as he was the most ingenious. Hubert had the shot of the day. He wanted us to hit left-handed with a right-handed club out of a small patch of water! The end result was that we were relaxed and were laughing so hard that nothing that happened the next day was going to faze us. I found doing this really relaxed us and helped our games in that we weren't tense when the tournament started. We all ended up playing well in that tournament, and I know it's in part because of the fun we had that previous day. We also gave some people in the gallery some interesting memories to take home with them.

RHYTHM

One drill for rhythm was to stand at the tee and hit balls with my feet together. The reason why this was so important was it taught me how to be in balance at all times off the tee. If I had my feet together and I swung wildly from my heels, I'd fall down. I would also practice with a radio playing, so as to be steady regardless of the music. I was always in balance, even when the music might take my mind off the game. It forced me to stay in focus.

Lee's philosophy was that kids have a great touch because they don't try to swing hard. The reason they don't try to swing hard is that they can't because they just don't have the raw power, and so they make up fun games with the short-game aspect of golf. By making up these games, their short game gets perfected, and when they grow and can pound the ball off the tee, their short game is already built upon good golf foundations, and they're ready for competitive play. Kids at the clubs are chipping and putting, not standing around hitting three-woods. Adults think only about power and driving the ball 300 yards, and they get neither distance nor accuracy. In tennis, kids would rather slice the ball and make it just drop once it makes it over the net. Kids playing tennis don't care about serving 150 miles per hour like Andre Agassi because they can't serve that fast, and so they have fun with the game and they allow the force to come later.

CHIPPING

Buster Bishop taught me much about chipping during my college days, and he had his own techniques. He was terrific at showing you a technique and getting you to believe in it and to use it effectively in your game.

One technique, in particular, that Coach Bishop taught us was how to chip from the fringe of the green. He called it the "chip and run." The drills taught us how the direction of the chip went through the air versus how it would end up rolling once on the ground. The drill was done using a five-iron. Coach Bishop made us use a five-iron, a six-iron, and a seven-iron. Coach Bishop is a genius in my book. The whole point of the drill was to prove that when you use a five-iron one-fourth of the total distance of the chip is in the air and three-fourths of the total distance is the roll on the green.

When you perform the drill with a six-iron you find the results slightly different. One-third of the total chipping distance off a six-iron is in the air and two-thirds of the total distance is the roll on the ground. Coach Bishop would then have us take out our seven-irons.

A seven-iron illustrates how important chipping is to the game of golf and how it can save your game and help you make birdie or save par. A seven-iron chip from the fringe of the green will have 50 percent of the total chipping distance in the air and 50 percent of the total distance on the ground in the form of the "roll." We worked with these three irons, and it made the difference in our game. That's why when I arrived on the PGA TOUR scene I was one of the few guys who knew fractional distance with regard to various aspects of the game of golf. From that first drill onward in college, I called my coach "One-third, two-thirds!"

Here it is, plain and simple. If you pace off forty feet from the cup, to the fringe around the green, and practice this drill using a five-iron, you will not only get the feel of your irons down perfectly but will also get that ball to roll closer to the "apple barrel," as Buster used to say. Buster had so many great expressions, and when he gave a golf class his voice carried forever. Because he had that booming voice, you heard that famous expression of his nice and loud, "One-third, two-thirds, got it?"

BUNKER PRACTICE

Lee and I practiced bunker shots together for hours. I would be in the bunker and he would make me create hard shots for myself. We'd hit balls into the bunker to give me a chance to get "out" from different lies in that trap. I used different clubs as well. I did not just go into the beach with my sand wedge and blast out, and for good reason. I used to blast out with an eight-iron in order to make sure that when the games counted and I went in there with my sand wedge, it would be easy. It's analogous to the baseball player swinging weighted bats in the on-deck circle. When he approaches the plate, suddenly his bat feels light and he can generate more bat speed. The same principle applies in golf. If you can get out of the sand cleanly with an eight-iron, then the sand-wedge blast looks and feels like a joke shot. It's as

THE LONG AND THE SHORT OF IT

easy as pie after a while. You have trained your muscles to have the right muscle memory and to recall that muscle memory on demand. There is an indescribable feeling that comes with the perfect sand-wedge shot from the bunker, and your body will tell you when you have the shot down pat. The game I usually played in the bunker was I would not leave the bunker area until I made a certain amount of shots. When I say "made," I mean holed out. I stood in that bunker as a teenager and told myself that I would hole out ten shots, and I did just that or I wouldn't leave until I did. I did the same with chipping. To this day I practice in the bunkers with eight- and nine-irons because there is no better tune-up for a possible bunker shot than consistently holing balls with an eight-iron or a nine-iron. Once the round begins I know that if I'm in the sand, I'm getting out easily with my sand wedge and probably going to get the ball within three feet of the cup.

"21"

Lee and I used to play a game on the putting green called "21." We played this game a lot and it helped me improve my putting because, as a youngster, it was a fun way of practicing. Lee's games taught me an invaluable lesson: that practice doesn't have to be ordinary and boring. Practice can be fun if you have fun with the idea of practice.

The way "21" worked was in the same manner as the game of horseshoes. We would start off with two balls. I would putt my two balls, and then he would follow by putting his two balls. The closest ball to the hole received one point. If you lipped it out, you received three points. If you made the putt, you received five points. If he made a putt, and then I made my putt, I received double points instead of him receiving his five points. You had to hit twenty-one exactly. So, if you had nineteen points and then you holed a putt, you went over the twenty-one mark and your score went right back to zero.

The game was great because it employed strategy and honed my golf skills. The game taught me all about lag putting and about making the big putts when it counted. We played this game by the hour at Nakoma Golf Club. The pro shop was right in front of the putting green, and so when Lee didn't have much to do in the pro shop, he would play games with me. Lee was a fantastic putter, and I learned much of my putting technique and strategy from him.

PUTTING PRACTICE

Lee and I played an eighteen-hole round of putting on the putting green, and this was great because it not only did not reward me, it penalized me at every step short of a made putt. No matter where we each started putting, if we didn't make the putt, we had to take the ball back one club length from the hole. In other words, if I hit a forty-foot putt that stopped ten inches from the hole, I had to bring the ball back three feet. No matter where I hit the ball, I always had a three-foot putt left to make, and so it taught me not to miss those all-important three-foot putts. The only way not to be left with a three-foot putt was by holing out. This game really tested your internal fortitude because it made you grind hard on putts that had to be made without question. There was never an "easy" next putt. This game is a great one to teach your child how to read breaks in greens. Go to a green with a lot of break in it and play this game with your kid, or your friend, or whomever. The drill teaches you to be able to make a three-foot putt, even on a tough green, at all times. The golfer really gets to know how to stroke the ball and how to read greens and judge the speed of greens. Sometimes the greens had so much break in them that I never finished. This game is usually played for a reward (i.e., a dime per stroke). It makes it enjoyable. You might make a thirty-footer and the opponent might five-putt.

Another practice technique we used was as follows: Lee and I used to take balls around the practice green and throw them in all different sorts of lies. I used to have to pitch from the edge of the fringe, and it forced me to make decisions as to which club to pitch with or whether to pitch at all and just putt. By tossing some balls around the first fringe cut and experimenting using different clubs for pitch shots, or sometimes not going with a pitch shot at all, you learn golf strategy, which is an essential element of the short game.

We've talked about how important practicing your short game is, and these are just a few ways to make your practice sessions more enjoyable.

10. The Best in the Long

Driving is a tough part of golf. You need to be straight, but you also need distance. Calvin Peete was a great straight driver. He wasn't long, however. Today, the PGA TOUR has devised a formula that I love. It's called the Total Driving formula. It's terrific because it combines distance and accuracy. Thus, it rewards the straight golfer who drives the longest. Tiger Woods is a perfect driver. He's long and straight. David Duval is a perfect driver. He has length and accuracy as well. Greg Norman, when he was at the top of his game and was winning tournament after tournament, was a great combination driver. I was paired with him, and the one thing I noticed was how he combined length and accuracy. Jack Nicklaus always put the ball on the fairway when he needed to, and when he wanted to be long he could attack that ball and hit with the longest of the ball strikers.

Andy Bean was a fantastic driver. He was really long and really strong. Just a terrific combination driver. Arnold Palmer was a wonderful driver, and still is today. He has been overlooked on the list of greatest drivers of all time. He drives the ball beautifully. He has length and he never misses a fairway. From 1962 to the present, my list of the top 3 or 4 go-to guys would be Nicklaus, who won a staggering amount of victories in a seventeen-year period, Tiger Woods, and David Duval.

The two best iron players I've seen are Lanny Wadkins and Johnny Miller. Johnny was so great that his caddie would get pin distances in half yards for him. He was that precise. Johnny could take any iron out of his bag and get the ball close to the pin. Lanny was an excellent short- to middle-iron player. When both these men were good, they were really good. Both are extremely confident and very aggressive. I can honestly say that they never met a pin they didn't shoot at! When they were off, however, they were in big trouble. Never did I play with either of these men in a round of golf that they didn't hit at least one ball within two feet of the hole for a tap-in, and sometimes they'd do it three or four times in a round.

Jack Nicklaus gets the award for "Mr. Consistency." Even when he was off, his shots were always decent because of the ball placement. Jack has exceptional mental strength. He never shot at a pin he didn't feel comfortable shooting at, whereas Lanny would shoot at every pin. Jack Nicklaus's course management is probably better than anyone who's ever played. He knew when to be aggressive and when to be conservative. For example, at the TPC in Jacksonville, Florida, there are big undulations in the course. There are stretches of holes where there are deep swells and the pin is tucked in some little knoll. Jack wouldn't shoot at that pin. He'd play the high-percentage safe shot. Lanny would shoot straight at the pin and either hit an incredible shot three feet from the hole or miss the green. If Jack played that hole ten times he'd have ten pars. Lanny's style of golf would give him the following breakdown in ten times: three birdies, two pars, five bogies. Again, all because of style. When there's a small surface area at which to shoot, and you attack the pin, you're going to get hurt most of the time. The player who's thinking smart knows when to hit the aggressive shot and when to back off.

It's as if you were sitting at Walt Disney World in Orlando, with

Orlando being the fairway, and tried to hit a golf ball to Pensacola, with the latter being the hole. If you shot right at Pensacola, you'd either come up smelling like a rose or be crying because you're off the green. The smart play would be to hit toward Tallahassee and then putt right on through.

One memorable iron shot for me, was Robert Gamez's shot holing out from the eighteenth fairway to win at Bay Hill at the Nestlé Invitational. He used a seven-iron and eagled the hole!

David Duval won the British Open in 2001, and he has always played well enough to win. The key was that he played some great shots after he got into trouble. He was able to overcome some poor shots by following them up with terrific shots. This is what being a champion is all about, and this is the key to winning tournaments. The way I look at it is that everyone is going to hit some bad shots, but the key is to be able to follow the bad shots up with great ones, whether these great shots include hitting tremendous bunker shots or getting the ball on the green from the deep rough beside the fairway. This is the fine line between winning and finishing in the middle of the field. Don't compound your mistakes. During the course of a round the best players in the world hit poor shots. The great players like Tiger Woods, however, just don't hit them in a row. Tiger always makes the great shots when it counts, and that's why he's so incredible. David Duval made some miraculous shots in the British Open. The second shot on Sunday out of the rough at the fifteenth hole was the key to the tournament in my book. David hit that fantastic shot, and at that time he had a two-shot lead. That lead, however, could have disappeared in a heartbeat! He didn't let it happen, and he extended his lead to three shots. He didn't make many mistakes and was efficient with respect to course management.

Great iron players have a combination of great muscle memory, so as to repeat the swing, and the ability to fire at the pin under pressure. It's real easy to bail out and hit the ball twenty feet to the right of the hole, but it takes a real champion to go for it and win.

11. Some Long-Game Advice

One of the hardest things in the world to do is to sit back and analyze your own game. I think the tough part about this stems from honesty. You need to be honest with yourself and to see where the greatest improvement can be made to achieve the greatest personal satisfaction.

Golfers must be able to judge what their initial abilities are and then judge themselves over a period of ten or fifteen rounds of golf. I know that sounds like a lot of golf, but that is exactly what you need to do before you can really judge yourself. How many times did you hit the ball in green-side bunkers but didn't get it up and onto the green? How many times did you three putt? Did you three putt because you hit really bad long putts or because you missed a one-footer or two-footer? Did you read the greens poorly? These questions can all be answered if a person is willing to be honest with him or herself and to sit down and chart his or her game over the course of these rounds. It will show you *where* you need to improve your game. This is harder than simply saying, "I didn't putt well today," but it's a more accurate assessment. This technique can boost your confidence as well. A golfer may go out and hit thirteen really good drives but hit one out of bounds. She might say to herself that she "didn't drive very well," when in fact the opposite is true. Here she had thirteen great shots! Only one missed!

Self-assessment is the key to understanding your golf game. It's analogous to a corporation that buys another corporation—a corporate merger. You have to break things down in order to know how to fix accounting problems or other problems within the company you just bought. Let's say that Corporation A bought Corporation B. They obviously did so for a particular purpose. Corporation A acquired Corporation B because it knew B had some intrinsic value to it, but it was underperforming for some reason. CEOs don't agree to merge other corporations into their own because they want a decrease in net worth. Corporate executives are always looking at the bottom line. Corporations want to maximize potential, and they feel that they can do something positive with this other corporation that hasn't been done before and thus make their original corporation all the more powerful.

Now let's apply that principle to the game of golf. It may not seem as if they are related at first glance, but they are quite analogous upon further inspection. A particular round of golf may be summarized like a balance sheet. Your scorecard can be your friend in this case. You need to look over your entire eighteen-hole round to see where your deficiencies are and how to correct them. You should be able to chart your game to see where you broke down during the course of the round. It might have been off the tee. It might have been in the bunker, taking three strokes to get out of the sand. It might have been because you three-putted every single hole, or four putted every hole. Once you see where your breakdown is, you can fix it and then you'll be a better golfer.

Doing this won't take you long at all, and fixing your problems is easier than just continuing to struggle and not to have any fun playing. You might feel, however, from an ego standpoint, that you're failing, but once you understand your weaknesses the solution is clearer and nearer than ever before, and so is success. You'll be getting out of the bunker on one stroke, or you'll be two-putting all the time, or you'll be hitting straighter off the tee.

The principle is self-evident when it comes to the long-game phase of golf. This is one of the most critical parts of the game. It is in the long game that the table is set for the entire hole. You are your own destiny maker here, and you should try and make it a good destiny. Give yourself the best start so as to par or birdie the hole. Remember one very important principle every time you address the ball from that little tee. The idea is a rather simple one, but it's worth stating again and again.

You don't have to use a driver off each tee. The key is finding a club you can hit in the fairway off the tee with. Good scores come easier from the fairway as opposed to the bushes!

For example, you might have a 400-yard par 4 with a lake on the right and bunkers on the left, and in between the lake and the bunkers is only about 20 yards wide. If you lay back at 250 yards the fairway might be 60 yards wide. I would approach that situation as follows. I would hit a three-wood short of that tiny area so that I would be hitting into the widest part of the fairway, and I would play a six-iron instead of a nine-iron. Having laid up short of all the trouble into the widest part of the fairway, you now give yourself the best opportunity to par the hole. You may not make as many birdies playing the hole this way, but you surely won't make as many bogeys or double bogeys.

If you used each method ten times, the one that will work best for making par or birdie consistently is the safe method. If you gamble maybe you could make an eagle, but you will certainly make a heck of a lot of double bogeys. I can guarantee you that much. This is a major reason why the average player throws so many shots away. They aren't good at looking at a hole and sizing up the situation for themselves and their own abilities.

Sometimes you might hit a five-iron off the tee to lay up and give yourself a great second six-iron shot. The logic most people employ is that they will "just" drive it down 210 yards in the air and just make it over that "stupid" lake without any problem. Well, the lake is smarter than the amateur playing the hole because nine times out of ten the amateur couldn't hit a ball 210 on the fly to save himself. The other players know it and the lake knows it, but the person hitting the ball doesn't know it. Why not be creative and hit a four-wood and a seven-iron?

The twelfth hole at the Masters is a great hole to further illustrate my point. The twelfth hole is a scenic par-3 hole. The hole plays 150 yards to the front of the green, and there is a huge bunker right in front of the green. When you approach the tee you should always be thinking what club you have in your bag that you can use to carry over that greenside bunker. You need to keep that 150-yard number in mind. The ball needs to carry over the bunker to get to the green. If the average guy steps up there and thinks that he'll just use an eight-iron and he can only hit an eight-iron 140 yards, the ball will always go into the bunker. Just try to block out the bunker and pick the club that goes 155 yards.

However, most of you reading are not PGA TOUR players. Keep that in mind and go with your own strengths and don't accentuate your weaknesses. Keep the focus on the distance to the hole, not on showing off to your friends or trying to use a club that will never allow the ball to carry over that big bunker to reach the green.

Having the proper outlook, to me, means learning control, both physical and mental. I can't stress that point enough. To enjoy this game, you must learn how to control the ball. If you can do this, you can play at any age. Just plunk it down the fairway, hit it up on the green, and lay the ball into the cup and make par. If you're in the woods, in lakes, or out of bounds, then it's harder to make par.

Not enough people understand the principle of knowing the contents of your golf bag and your own physical limitations. You, the golfer, must know how far you—not your buddy, but you—can hit each one of your clubs. It doesn't matter how far these young great tour golfers today hit their irons, it's how far you can hit *your* three-wood or seven-iron.

There are a lot of people who walk up to a hole, look at their partner, and use the same numbered iron or type of club that the partner uses. That's the wrong approach.

As you become a better player and you're more consistent with your game, go to the range and really play each club to get an average distance for each one. Hit twenty-five balls with a sand wedge and see how far the average ball goes, not the longest shot but the average shot. Then tell yourself "I'm this type of player with the sand wedge," weather conditions being constant. If the average wedge shot goes 100 yards, then you are a 100-yard wedge player. Repeat this process for each club. Then when you're out on the golf course and you're standing next to the 175-yard sprinkler marker, you know you're a three-iron, not a five-iron! You then pull out your 175-yard club versus another club. If you've got a 160-yard shot, and you know you can't hit a ball with a seven-iron more than 150 yards, then you're not going to make the shot with your seven-iron, even if your buddy can overshoot the hole with a seven-iron. Time to take out your six-iron!

Park your ego and select the club that's right for you. Who cares if you're hitting a three-iron and your buddy is hitting a five-iron! If you can hit it closer than he or she can, that's all that's important.

When we have these corporate outings, I tell the women not to be intimidated by the men because the odds are that the women will hit the ball closer to the pin because they're playing the game like it should be played instead of playing based upon ego, as many men do in the game of golf.

The object is to get the ball as close to the hole as possible, not to use the highest-numbered iron off the tee.

If you're on a par-5 and have a great lie on the fairway, and you're thinking about a three-wood or five-wood or three-iron because you can't get to the green, anyway, then that's a whole different story. Then it's a matter of judgment. I would suggest that if you know you cannot reach the hole and the difference is between ultimately hitting a nine-iron or a wedge third shot, then play based upon which club you'll ultimately feel comfortable with in the end. Play for the "shot" after this shot. Think ahead. Select the club that will set you up for the comfortable club on the next shot. If you're more comfortable with that three-wood, then use that club, especially if it will set you up for a shot with another comfortable club.

We'd all be better off if there weren't numbers on the clubs. You'd have a bag full of clubs and you'd have to hit shots with them and then you'd just write on the club "150-yard club" with a Magic Marker. We'd all be better off if we didn't put our egos in the bag along with the clubs!

If we all walked up to a par-3 hole and took out our 150-yard club, we'd be a lot better off, versus taking out the "numbered clubs," such as the three iron, the five iron, the seven iron. All this does is it gets us into the wrong frame of mind because we're no longer thinking about the best golf shot for us, we're thinking about our own little "egos." We're now more concerned with showing our friends that we can use the same clubs as they use and hit the ball a lot farther. The whole idea is to understand your talents and the level at which you can play the game, then to go out and play the game within your talents and not allow others to dictate how you play the game.

Another factor, which is often a distraction, is the scorecard. Instead of using it as a tool or a guide, some golfers get very compulsive about it. I personally haven't used a scorecard in more than twenty years insofar as to gauge my game. Too often, many golfers become mesmerized by their scorecards and look at them when they should just be concentrating on the hole on which they're playing. The scorecard is more of a hindrance than a help sometimes, especially when you're looking at it to see how many par-5 holes are left to make birdie on to help lower your score and meanwhile you mess up the easy par-3 hole on which you're playing.

You need to use the driving range to get the feel of your irons. You could hit off the tee, or off the grass, or whatever suits you. Just use each iron and find out your average distance from the tee and from the grass.

In fact, the perfect driving-range experience could be as follows: You go to your local driving range and you find a broken rubber tee there. You could also bring a rubber tee with you that you've sliced in half. The height of the tee is important. How you tee the ball at the driving range will be an important part of how your body is used to hitting the ball off the tee with that particular golf club. For all practical purposes the tees that are excessively long are useless to the average golfer. It doesn't do the golfer much good to practice with a five-iron off of a tee that's raised two inches above the ground.

Once at the driving range, you might want to work on your setup even if you never hit a ball that day. The setup is one phase of the game that you can learn even by watching golf on television. One of the things I like about Greg Norman's game is his setup. He has a terrific setup at the golf ball. It looks as if he is always square. He does a good job of keeping his back straight and he has excellent arm position. His arms are inside his shoulders, which in golf language means that he never lets his arms get too far away from his body. Greg does a tremendous job of keeping his arms in sync with his body. He keeps his arms close because of his setup. His elbows are always close to his rib-cage.

The proper use of irons is an important and fun part of the game of golf. In my opinion, you need to practice using them before you go out on the golf course. The perfect solution is to bring your own broken rubber tee and use that cut-down tee for your iron practice. It will be a more "true" shot and a better driving-range experience because it is this type of tee that you should use when you actually tee off.

I'm also often asked about grooves on irons wearing out. This does not automatically spell disaster. Sometimes a club without any grooves can allow the ball to spin just as beautifully as a club with unbelievable grooves. It's a misconception that needs to be addressed. Perfect grooves on an iron do help, but if you have a perfect lie and it's nice and dry outside, then the ball will stop. If there's moisture on the ground, your ball may not stop where you want it to even with perfect grooves. Moisture affects the golf ball just as throwing a knuckleball affects the baseball. If you throw a baseball without any spin, the path is unpredictable. That's why a hitter can't time his swing as easily as he could with a fastball or with a normal curveball. It's the same in the game of golf. If there's moisture between the golf ball and club face, then the path of the golf ball is rather uncertain. The golfer loses that coveted control aspect of his or her game.

I often get asked whether to tee the ball high or low when using irons at the driving range. I don't think the height of the tee should vary when you play a round of golf. If you tee too high, the ball will be undercut and won't travel far. If you tee too low, you might hit the ground first before hitting the ball.

I feel that a player needs to tee the ball so that it sits just above the tops of the blades of grass. This will enable you to make a good iron swing and to develop a muscle memory for the next time you use that particular iron. Moving the ball up and down won't allow you the consistency that is so crucial to the game of golf.

The lie of the ball is crucial to the club selection and the type of shot you want to play. If the ball is sitting in a depression or in a mower's cut, then this situation will affect the club selection, so don't use only one type of iron at the driving range, because many times the lie of the ball in an actual game will dictate the situation, and if you've practiced with only one type of iron, then you won't be able to hit the shot properly. It helps to practice getting out of divots and odd lies for this very reason. You will get many unusual lies on the golf course. The more you can practice these lies, the better your game will be in the end. If you're in a divot, you can't use the normal shot that you'd use off a perfect lie.

So much of the driving range is to re-create situations that you would actually encounter on the golf course. One such situation is the one I discussed in the introductory paragraph on the long game. If there is a fairway lie and you choose to use a wood rather than an iron, do not take a divot. Fairway woods don't take divots. They are meant to sweep the ball off the fairway and onto the green. Irons are made to take the big divots. This is important to remember because the conception of taking a divot at all times is another fallacy in golf. The fairway woods don't take the divots that the irons take because the club is designed for distance and loft. The club face is designed to sweep across the blades of fairway grass gently, and the natural makeup of the club will do the rest of the work in making sure that the ball carries far. You should practice using your woods at the driving range as well because often enough you will have to use a five-wood off the tee, and you most always will need, during the course of a round of golf, your three-wood off the tee.

You should practice chip shots at the range as well. You should practice using your high-numbered irons off the mat and imagine you are aiming for different markers. You should also practice fade shots and slices as well. Practice hooking the ball and slicing it at imaginary points. Just make the situation at the driving range as close to the real thing as possible. You are trying to re-create actual golf situations. You're not trying to hit the ball left-handed when you're right-handed. You're not trying to do crazy things. You are trying to imagine a nice par-3 hole right in front of you that plays about 150 yards. You should want to approach the tee shot with the same club that you would use on the golf course. You should also use the driving range to improve on your mid-iron shots by really pinpointing how far you hit each iron on average. The last tip of mine for the driving range is to use your driver judiciously. Try and maximize the speed you can generate with the trunk of your body.

Remember, the range is a tune-up for the golf course. Oh, yes. Have fun while you're there.

CLUBS

As for buying the right kind of clubs, especially drivers and woods, here is some advice. When golf pros talk about clubs, they often neglect to explain to the general public the true significance of the word *club*. The game of golf may be, from an equipment standpoint, broken down as follows: woods, irons, sand wedge, pitching wedge, and putter. Both woods and irons have shafts, grips, and faces. I've looked inside the golf bags on tour, and this is what I've found to be the case as of the year 2001.

On the PGA TOUR today, many players who tried graphite-shafted clubs have since returned to steel, especially in their irons! You might actually find some golfers using woods made from wood. Woods can be made out of wood, titanium, metal, graphite, and plastic composite heads.

The faces of the clubs, however, vary greatly. Some players have steel-shafted irons with club faces that are composed of titanium, whereas other players have steel-shafted irons with forged metal faces. Each golf equipment company uses a slightly different alloy blend to try and achieve the best face result. Every company wants to claim it has the best face.

Whether you are a beginning golfer or a great golfer, when you finally make the big decision to go out and buy that set of golf clubs you've been eyeing, I've got some advice for you. If you're an advanced golfer, go to a good driving range, with a good pro shop, and they will have a setup by Calloway, Titleist, Cleveland Golf, or Wilson, where you can pick from different lengths and weights. Then, take those clubs down to the practice range and test them! Make sure you are allowed to test the clubs. If you are unable to do so, do not buy the clubs from that establishment. You must be able to test your clubs. Once you've tested the clubs and have found a shaft that has worked for you, then compare companies (whether it be Callaway, Adams, Wilson, Cleveland Golf, Titleist, Ping, Taylor, etc.) and see which make works best for you, given comparable feel and grip and weight.

For the beginner, I think you're better off buying a good quality set of used clubs versus a brand-new set of off-name or sport shop type line. Buy a set of used Calloway clubs or some other brand-name clubs that work for you rather than a new set of your favorite brand.

You might wonder why I suggest buying a good set of used clubs rather than a cheap new set. Plain and simple, and contrary to some popular belief, a used set is nothing more than a great set of clubs hit a few more times. A set of golf clubs that's four or five years old doesn't mean they're not going to work. Find a good set of used clubs after you've tested out different shafts and weights. It may be as simple as buying a used set of clubs, replacing the grips with brand-new grips. Then the clubs look brand-new!

My first set of clubs was a beginner's set of clubs. Then I progressed to a lady's club! I used a lady's shaft in my Wilsons because as a teenager I needed a softer shaft. As I grew and became stronger, I kept with Wilson equipment and progressed to a men's shaft. The sets were all basically the same, throughout my progressions, but the shafts were different. I used the men's shaft for a while and then progressed to a stiff men's shaft, then finally to the extra-stiff men's shaft, the PGA tour type. I used the same set of irons for both of my U.S. Open championships, the Wilson staff set! I still have that set today, and I've been experimenting with other clubs as well.

Clubs are extremely personal items. What could be good for your buddy may not be good for you. Two people can have the most ardent discussion over which set of clubs is "the best," and there isn't any right answer. The only right answer is the set that feels good to you. That's why it's important to test the clubs. You might find one set of clubs that is ugly to the eye, yet they work perfectly for you. That's the set you should buy, not for aesthetic reasons but because they do the job for you.

Let's say there's a new golfer who's been playing for two years and that golfer is a thirty-six handicap. That golfer should not be going out and buying the latest driver for three or four hundred dollars. That's not going to make that golfer a ten handicap. Everybody thinks that with fifty extra yards their game will dramatically improve. The only way to get better is to take lessons and practice. Then when their handicap is in that twenty range, the extra yards may help some in the long run.

In 2001, I signed a deal with Calloway Golf, so I officially endorse Calloway Clubs. Ely Calloway was a great man. He single-handedly created the Big Bertha, which revolutionized the driving aspect of golf. The Big Bertha gave us all distance with a comfortable feel. It's a club that anyone can use and feel comfortable with, as far as I'm concerned. Then Mr. Calloway introduced us to the titanium heads, which gave us an even bigger sweet spot on the face of the club and even more distance.

When I learned of Mr. Calloway's passing I was sad not only because of my relationship with him, but I felt sad for the game of golf. Calloway Golf was more than just a company. It represented a modern new millennium in golf club manufacturing that changed golf much like Gene Sarazen did when he invented the sand wedge.

Then comes the selection of the putter. Putters are so different nowadays that selecting a putter can be enjoyable but difficult because of all of the models from which to select. It's difficult to find a putter that you are comfortable with, and everyone is searching for that perfect putter. That's why golfers try out many putters before they find the right one for them.

Everybody wants to be an exceptional golfer without spending the time on that journey. Half the fun is the journey! Many times a top player will talk about how much fun it was to get to being number one in the world and when they got there it wasn't that much fun. Going from a twenty to a fourteen to a ten is the fun. People need to understand the concept of "the journey" in golf, and then they will enjoy the game more and have better results on the course.

12. Where the Short Game All Begins

Just what is the "short game?" The short game in my book is any shot less than 125 yards to the hole. A tour player within 125 yards will use either the sand wedge or some other lofted wedge, such as the pitching wedge. Obviously, putting is a great part of the short game, and perfecting the use of the putter and its pendulum motions is important.

Putting is so crucial to winning in golf. For successful putting, judging the slope of the green is vitally important. There is also the question of grain on the green, and being able to judge the speed of the green is critical.

Ball position in your stance is so important when it comes to the short game. You should position yourself such that you have the ball in the middle of your stance. Now that you've got the ball positioned properly, the important thing to realize in actually hitting this shot is that you should probably use a three-quarter-length swing and accelerate the club through the hitting area. The biggest problem most players have with short shots is that their swing is too long and they decelerate, which can lead to bad results.

Reading greens is a science. To be able to read the green and to figure out how much break you're going to have you must understand at what speed you're going to hit the putt, and too often you'll see amateurs hit putts that run right by the hole, almost over the hole, and then pass the hole by ten feet. In their minds they've hit a good putt just because the ball almost hit the hole.

They did not make a good putt at all. If they had hit the ball with the correct speed and they ended up just pulling the ball three feet left of the hole, instead of missing the hole by inches and having the ball run by the hole, they would have been in better position. Most amateurs don't think that the putt that stops three feet to the left of the hole is a good putt at all, but it is a good putt because they've judged the speed properly. If you don't know how hard you're going to hit your putt, you don't know how to judge how much the putt will break.

An example of this is that you have a ten-foot putt in front of you. You hit the ball. The first ball dies at the hole. It might break one foot. The second putt might go two feet by the hole and break in front six inches. The only way to make putts is to figure out not just the speed of the green, but the break.

If you know you can judge this idea of speed perfectly all the time, it makes the green easier to read. You know in your mind how much the ball is going to break from looking at the green, and you know how hard you will hit the ball. You can take the same putt and hit it where the ball dies at the hole, and it might break one foot. You might hit a putt where it goes two feet by the hole and it only breaks six inches. Knowing the strength you'll need to employ to successfully putt the ball is a combination of a lot of different facets of the game, such as the slope and the firmness of the green and the effect of weather conditions.

You hear the players talk about how at one tournament their speed was great and so they made a lot of putts. The next week you'll see the players shake their heads in disbelief that they just couldn't get the speed right and missed the putts they were making the previous week.

Then there is the situation as to whether to ask your caddie for help. It's a personal question, and some players do ask their caddies to line up their putts and help them judge the speed of the green and the breaks in the green. I personally don't speak to my caddie on putts. Most of the time it's visualizing the situation on your own that matters, because you're the only one who knows the speed you want to pick.

I have always felt that figuring out the break is something that the player has to do on their own. The best putters don't ask for a lot of help from their caddies. I always believed I know the speed of the putt better than the caddie. Sometimes caddies offer too much information and too much help.

In trying to better learn the short game, I always paid attention to the other golfers on the tour particularly when I first started. I tried to play practice rounds with better players so that I could watch them and see what they did in their short game. I tried to play practice rounds with guys like Gene Littler, Charles Coody, Lou Graham, and Bob Murphy. I wanted their input and experience on wedge shots, putting, and reading greens. I enjoyed watching these men prepare. Everyone can learn from someone else, and watching these guys helped me a great deal.

13. Out of the Bunker and onto the Green

BUNKER SHOT

- Sand wedge important
- Has "bounce" because of flange
- Mid to forward of stance
- Aim left about 20°
- Club face open
- Two inches behind ball
- Accelerate through swing

The greenside bunker shot is the only shot in the world where you don't have to hit the ball! Just think about it. Here you are in the bunker and suddenly you're thinking, "Andy says don't hit the ball. What in the world is he talking about?"

The idea is that you're not hitting the ball. When you are in a greenside bunker the only way to get out successfully is to think about hitting the sand behind the ball. You're trying to have the club enter the sand anywhere from one to three or four inches behind the ball. If you miss by one inch and hit two inches behind the ball instead of three inches behind the ball, the ball still comes out cleanly. If you miss a driver or a five iron by an inch, you might miss the ball. In actuality, the bunker shot is one of the easiest shots to make if you're not scared to death of actually hitting it. You get the right equipment, the right technique, and a little bit of confidence, and it thus becomes a relatively easy shot. Most tour players would rather have the ball in the bunker than in the rough around the green.

The whole idea in perfecting these bunker shots is to go to a greenside bunker and practice getting out by hitting two inches behind the ball with your sand wedge. There is a feel to planting your feet and having the ball between your feet off the middle of your stance. Then you swing the club and aim about two inches behind the ball. The grains of sand fly up and the ball pops out onto the green, and everybody thinks you're a pro.

The greenside bunker shot must be practiced by everyone because it's an aspect of golf that keeps on repeating itself. You will seldom go through a round of golf and not hit one greenside bunker. Rather than saying, "Woe is me," you will be able to go into that bunker and get your ball out on the first try.

For me, the bunker shot was a lot of fun as a kid and is still a fun shot to this day. As a kid I spent a great many hours in the bunker practicing and perfecting bunker shots. I truly enjoyed it. I would make up games where I would try to hole a specific amount each day before I'd quit practicing. Some days were longer than others.

My father and Lee Milligan are responsible for my short-game success. My dad gave me the initial coaching I needed, and then when I progressed he approached Lee Milligan. Lee had a fabulous short game, and he was an excellent chipper, sand wedge player, and putter. He loved to teach the short game because he was so good at it. He also knew how to teach it. We spent a lot of time in the bunker and on the greens perfecting chipping, bunker shots, and putting. When you're at a time in your golfing life where your friends are hitting drivers and you're putting and chipping, the dividends pay off later on in your golfing life.

Lee always explained why things needed to be done, and that was what I liked most about him as a teacher. He made it a big point to tell me that I needed to get a sand wedge with the right kind of bounce on it, whereas other young kids would just go into the bunker with a pitching wedge. Back then all there was in the way of sand wedges was the 56-degree sand wedge. Because a club has to fit properly, Lee made sure that he got me set up correctly.

When most people would see their ball land in the sand, they'd emotionally just give up and want to quit for the day. Not me. I enjoyed the thrill of being in the bunker. I always felt that if I could get good lift on the ball, I'd get it right near the hole. Repetition of solid performances is the key to success in anything one does in life. You've got to be able to make the bunker shot again and again and again. It all comes with practice and with the right attitude in practice, which will build the proper muscle memory. Getting out of a bunker must become almost second nature for you. A similar outlook applies to other sports.

Routines are fine and dandy, but they need to last ten seconds, not ten minutes and ten seconds! These experts on golf give people pregame routines that are so involved that it would make any normal person want to quit the game of golf. Fuzzy Zoeller and Lanny Wadkins have pregame routines. They last ten seconds. They don't stand there looking at their right forearm and doing exercises with golf clubs.

Lance Armstrong, the cyclist, doesn't tell himself to pedal with his left foot, then right foot, then left foot. His mind just knows that this is going to be the routine when he rides in the Tour de France.

All of the articles that talk about the pregame routine before you hit the shot fail to mention that you can't consciously be thinking about your shoulders or your hands while you're playing. Many players get in trouble when they think too much. Tour players may think about the *type* of shot that they want to play out of the bunker. This is not the same as the technical aspects of playing the bunker. They're not thinking about their shoulders or hands. They're merely thinking about the specific shot they're going for in that given situation.

If you're scared to death of bunker shots, you'll never practice them.

The first thing to do along your way to mastering bunker shots is to find yourself a good sand wedge. It's the bounce on the sand wedge that keeps the club from digging into the sand and lets it skip across the top layer of sand, which is why it's easy to hit the ball out of the bunker. Most people play bunker shots with the club face square or closed because they think that's what they're supposed to be doing. It's the opposite. You need to have your club face as open as possible so that the club face accentuates the bounce, making the club work better. When Gene Sarazen invented the sand wedge it was to achieve this bounce that I speak of today.

Again, all you need to do is bring the club through the ball by hitting a couple of inches behind the ball. If you accelerate your swing, the ball will come out cleanly every time. If an amateur gains some confidence by making a bunker shot, suddenly the golf world seems a whole lot brighter. What was the hardest shot suddenly becomes easy.

What happens if your balls buries itself in the bunker? You have to adjust your normal thinking. Instead of the club face open, here you want to close the club face. This helps the dig into the sand, which helps the ball pop out without any spin, so the ball will run instead of stopping.

What do you do if your ball is against the face of a bunker? Sometimes you have to pitch out sideways. Forget about being a hero and go into damage control. We see countless examples at the British Open of steep-faced bunkers. One I well remember was in 2000, when David Duval hit it in the pot bunker at seventeen at St. Andrews. He had trouble, but he learned how to approach those bunkers, and he came back in 2001 and he won the British Open.

There is also a distinction between greenside bunkers and fairway bunkers. The stance you use when hitting out of a fairway bunker is the same stance you would use if you were hitting on the fairway. However, you want the ball further back toward your right foot. The reason you do this is so that you will hit the ball first, eliminating the possibility of fat shots.

Two of the greatest bunker players I've had the chance to play with are Chi Chi Rodriquez and Gary Player. Yet these two great bunker players use different techniques. Chi Chi has a handsy swing with the club face wide open. Gary, on the other hand, uses arms and shoulders in swinging the club with the club face square.

One thing they have in common is that they both have great confidence in the sand and get great results.

All players have become better bunker players because of the sand wedge revolution. Years ago you had a sand wedge and a pitching wedge. Today there are a plethora of sand wedges with different lofts, ranging from forty-nine degrees to sixty-five or seventy degrees. This has increased bunker play accuracy.

Amateurs should try these new clubs to gain some confidence in their own game. The four or five degrees of more loft really can help your game in many ways. Every player on tour now carries three wedges in their bags. Every once in a while I'll spot a player with four wedges in his or her bag. Specialization in clubs has become so prevalent that players have clubs for specific shots and situations.

There has been great golf drama from the bunker in recent years. One memorable bunker shot that stands out in my mind was when Bob Tway beat Greg Norman by holing the bunker shot on the last hole of the 1986 PGA Championship at Inverness in Toledo, Ohio. That was a dramatic way to win a major. He won the whole tournament by making this unbelievably picturesque bunker shot. Anyone who says bunker shots are not high drama is wrong. Some of the greatest of emotions have come from those sandy beaches right along-side those beautiful greens.

I've been very proud of a couple of bunker shots I've played. I hit two bunker shots to win both U.S. Opens. My first great bunker moment came at the eighteenth hole at Cherry Hills on Sunday in 1978, and the other bunker moment came at the seventeenth hole at Oakland Hills on Saturday in 1985.

I firmly believe kids, or any beginning golfer, should have fun with the game first and foremost. Make up little games from the bunker. Pretend there's a ball on the green and it's Jack Nicklaus's shot. Then hit your shot to beat Jack! We all have beaten Palmer and Nicklaus in our minds millions of times growing up. Then, of course, those of us who have been privileged enough to play with these two icons realize quickly that our childhood games were just that—games. My child-hood pals and I used to make up games and have fun to see who could hit the ball closest to the hole or who could putt the ball so many times in a row in from three feet.

14. Chipping

Chipping is another fundamental part of golf that is inescapable.

The most important aspect to chipping is understanding what you're trying to accomplish. The obvious answer is to get the ball as close to the hole as possible. However, most amateur golfers don't know how to go about achieving this goal. The most important lesson when it comes to chipping is to learn to use a lot of different clubs around the green. Use one technique and use different clubs to make the ball go different distances and stop in different manners.

Chipping is a lot about being comfortable with your stance and with your setup for the shot. Most players on the tour play the chip shot from an open stance. You might put more weight on your left foot than in other shots, but the setup must be solid. You need to use good fundamentals, such as a lot of arms and not much hands. I try to chip the ball much like my pendulum putting stroke, without a lot of extra movement. The whole key to chipping is practice! It is one area of the game in which fast improvement can come to you, but you must practice all the time. You need to go to a practice green and spend some time creating the type of chip shots that you will likely encounter on the golf course. I would recommend practicing chipping from five feet off the green and then from fifteen feet off the green, chipping from both distances to the same hole. This way you will learn both the stroke and the type of shot. You will also learn how to execute the same shot with different clubs. This was something which both Lee Milligan and Coach Bishop taught me, as I spoke about before. I called Buster "One-third, two-thirds" because he made me understand the relationship between using an iron to chip and how far that ball will carry in the air, then how far it would roll along the green.

Some people will have different stances. Some will stand upright and others will stand bent. Some players choke up on the club and some do not. The whole key to chipping is that there is no one correct stance for the chip shot, but there is one pervasive idea throughout everyone's game, and that is the idea of keeping the rhythm consistent and being able to repeat your technique.

The chip and run from seven to eight feet off the green is almost the same stroke you would use if you were using a putter. The idea to always keep in the back of your mind is that the longer the ball is in the air, the harder it is to control. The pitching wedge is not to be used for pitching all the time. It's merely another club in your bag. I can't stress this enough to the average weekend golfer. It's a misconception to use this club labeled *P* all the time. Don't do it. You need to take the amount of fringe the ball must carry over and the length of the green to the pin into account when selecting your club. An example of this is that you're six feet off the green and there's thirty feet of fringe to carry over. If you use a six-iron and carry that shot into the green, it will roll way past the hole. This is a situation where you need to take your pitching wedge or sand wedge and lob the ball into the green so that it will stop.

The great chippers and pitchers around the green have a lot of imagination to create shots. Seve Ballesteros was the best at making up shots around the green. Seve could get out of trouble like no other. He used a wide variety of clubs and used them all well. He could have a perfect chip shot using any club from any distance around the green. He was relaxed and in control, and he let the club and his natural chipping stroke do the work for him.

The way I love to practice chip shots is to go to the golf course early in the morning or late at night. This allows me to re-create chip shots from around the green that you get on the golf course in real situations. This type of practice eliminates the element of surprise in a real game.

Let's say there's a situation on the golf course where you have twenty yards of green with which to work, and your ball is five feet off the front of the green. In this situation you might choose to chip that ball onto the green with a four- or five-iron! You want the ball low, onto the green, and then running. You would never want to hit that shot using a wedge.

In the course of a round of golf, I might chip with anything from a four-iron to a sand wedge. As a matter of fact, some guys today even use fairway woods to chip in some situations. You can chip the ball with pretty much every single club in your bag at some point in time.

The chip shot, or the pitch shot, requires a considerable amount of mental preparation. Just because you're not on the green doesn't mean you can't make the shot and put that ball right into the hole. Most people are afraid of messing up as opposed to looking at the shot in a positive manner. Many times a chip shot three feet off the green is a better shot than a ball placed right in the center of the green forty feet from the hole, which may be positioned at the far end of the green.

WHAT ARE THE PROPER CHIPPING TECHNIQUES

The chipping motion comes from turning the V that is created between the shoulders and hands.

Most people use too much movement in their hands and wrists when they chip. There are three no-nos that people still seem to do: (1) too much use of hands and wrists, (2) too big a backswing, resulting in deceleration during their contact swing, or (3) trying to help the ball up in the air by lifting it with their club, and so they are really scooping it.

Those three mistakes are the components of bad chipping and result in higher scores at the end of the round. The simple way to become a better chipper is to eliminate your hands from the stroke. Grip the club and create a triangle between the club and your two shoulders. You want to turn that triangle back, then accelerate through with that triangle so as to eliminate a lot of hand movement. In doing this, you keep the backswing a little bit shorter and you accelerate through, and all of a sudden you'll hit the ball nice and solid all of the time. You'll get the ball up in the air and you won't have to try and help it up or scoop it up.

We've got the situation where the ball has rolled near the green. Most players will want to try to putt this ball, because it is so very close to the green. However, there is enough grass around the ball so that the grass will get between the ball and the club face of the putter, which will cause the player to lose control of that shot. The better players will take a sand wedge and will try to top or belly the shot, which is done by hitting the middle of the ball with the very leading edge of the sand wedge—not the face of the wedge but its leading edge. What this will do is cut through those blades of grass. You'll hit the ball solidly, and it will roll off beautifully just as is you'd putted it from the green.

Another type of shot you see the players play a lot in major tournaments is where the ball is in the really deep grass around the green. They will take a sand wedge, make a great big swing, and hit the ball as if it were a bunker shot. They are hitting behind the ball and the ball flops up in the air. I call it the "flop shot," and recently Phil Mickelson has made this shot his trademark. This is a great U.S. Open shot because the grass is so thick and long around the green that you can't chip the ball with a seven-iron.

Raymond Floyd and Hubert Green are all living proof that in golf you do not have to do things the same way as others to be successful. Their styles are drastically different when it comes to pitching. Hubert Green hunches down and chokes up on the club. He also uses quite a bit of hands in his pitching motion. Raymond Floyd stands tall and uses more arms in his pitching motion. They both achieve the same results.

I said before that amateurs should eliminate use of hands in pitching and now I'm praising Hubert Green for his great pitching and use of hands. Here's the reason. If the average guy wants to use a lot of hands, then fine. Go ahead and hit *five hundred* chips every day for the next thirty years and you'll be able to do it! If you want to be a good chipper and you play twice a week, once a week, or once every two weeks, then you need to eliminate your hands from chipping.

Some great chipping moments in golf have come in some interesting situations. Tom Watson, in the 1982 U.S. Open at Pebble Beach, on the seventeenth hole Sunday, chipped the ball into the hole and assured himself a U.S. Open victory. This was probably one of the greatest chip shots of all time in modern golf. This was a major championship, with major pressure on Tom, yet he did it. The heart of a true champion is that will to win, and Tom had it that day.

Lee Trevino chipped in to win the 1972 British Open against Tony Jacklin. He hit the ball over the green, flubbed a chip, then chipped the next shot in for birdie.

Larry Mize had a memorable chip shot to win the 1987 Masters on the second hole of sudden-death, the eleventh hole, beating Greg Norman.

Tiger Woods made a fantastic chip at Muirfield on the 14th hole. He hit the ball over the green and then chipped in to win the British Open.

Payne Stewart hit a miraculous chip shot on the 72nd hole of the tournament at Pinehurst in 1999 to assure himself the 1999 U.S. Open Championship.

The reason why many fans don't remember more great chipping moments in golf history is because they're just not shown on television. There is a misconception in the media that anybody on tour can hit a nice chip shot, whereas hitting a one-iron is a tough feat. It's just not true. Chipping is not an easy task, and when it's done beautifully it deserves some attention. If you are a golfer who shoots in the hundreds, the most important area to practice is chip shots within fifty yards to the green.

15. My Putting Story

Putting is a very individual part of the game of golf. You see a lot of different styles from some of the best players, but the two things they have in common are good putters and the ability to swing the putter back in line and accelerate it forward so that the line always keeps the club face square at contact. Most good putters use a lot of arms and shoulders in their putting strokes. Remember, the most important thing is that you have to accelerate through the ball. In today's game, the golf course conditions are so good that putting the ball is an important aspect of the game. This putting technique works both for putting the ball from the fairway or from the fringe.

I have never been a great putter, even as a kid. I was a great ball striker, but not a great putter. I tried all sorts of putters and grips. I tried putting cross-handed and that didn't work. I tried all sorts of experiments long before it was chic to experiment. My judgment of speed was lacking, and it wasn't until my sophomore year in college when things changed for me. I saw this putter in a junk store and bought it for two dollars. It was this Spalding Cash-In, which I fiddled around with. It caused me to change my style to where I choked up a lot on the putter. By choking up on the putter it helped me to judge the speed of my putts a whole lot better. My junior year in college I had the best year of golf, winning tournaments left and right and making the big-time putts. Both U.S. Opens were won with that putter. The faster the greens, the better I putted. It was the best two-dollars I ever invested!

It was simply amazing how the putter changed me. As I said, for years and years I stood up over putts much the way Ray Floyd does, and although I could get the line of the ball down pat, my speed wasn't very good. The greatest misconception for most amateurs is that the technique of putting rests in the line of the putt. Most golfers think that if they get the ball near the hole, they've hit a good putt. Speed, however, is the most important aspect of putting. You must be able to judge the speed of the green, or else you won't be able to judge the breaks in the green.

So a junk-store putter allowed me to feel comfortable enough to where I developed my unorthodox crouch, where I look as if I'm bent in half when I'm set to the ball on the green. I suddenly found my golf balls were heading in the right direction and were stopping within the right distance from the cup. I stayed with that technique and use it to this very day on the tour. Because my hands were taken out of the stroke, and I used my shoulders and arms a lot more, I suddenly had control of the putt.

Putters, however, are another conundrum when it comes to buying them based on what is seen on television. The difference between putters is going to be negligible if the amateur is a good putter. That person will be able to putt with anything. If the person is a crummy putter, no putter will help their game. The difference between putters is the look of the putter. If you were to put a tennis shoe on the end of a broomstick, there would be a PGA player who could make birdie after birdie with this device, such as Loren Roberts and Brad Faxon.

The other important aspect to putting, once you've found the right putter, is reading greens with regard to speed and being able to control your putter accordingly. It's amazing that ball speed can be so crucial in the short game, but it is crucial. If you can make a thirty-three-foot putt go thirty feet, even though you're three feet off line, you're still only three feet from the hole. You'll be in great position to finish the hole on the very next putt, having only a three-foot putt to finish. The person who "goes for it" and lines it up perfectly only to see the ball miss the hole by inches and roll down the green twelve feet, however, runs the risk of not making that second putt. He still has a twelve-foot putt to make on his second shot, whereas the person with the poor line and the proper ball speed has only a three-foot putt to make on her second shot. The player who judged the speed of the green properly is going to have a lower score on his golf card at day's end.

The long putter is something that I just can't use at all. I don't care how long a putter is, but I don't think it should be braced against your body. I think the kids today would be better putters if they used the long putters. What the long putters do is take the hands out of the putting stroke, thus forcing a pendulum motion, which is the proper motion for putting. However, if you weren't allowed to brace it against your body, I don't think anyone would use it because it would be hard to control. I think it's not really a stroke if the club is braced against your body. The USGA can't legislate the length of the golf club, but it could forbid a player to brace the club against the body.

I was out one day trying to explain to my wife, Susan, how to get the sense of feel and speed. It's almost as if you're trying to take the ball and toss it with your hand at the hole. In other words, it's as if you paced off fifteen feet from the hole and elected to toss the ball underhand into the hole. Your mind would immediately register a sensory impulse to your arm, which would enable you to gauge the proper rhythm and motion. Your arm would suddenly have the right feel, and the result of that proper feel would be a ball tossed at a proper speed necessary to get the ball in the hole. The same principle applies to putting, only now you have the putter in your hand instead of just tossing the ball. The putter is an extension of your arm. You then take hold of your putter and now the head of the club, instead of your hand, will do the work in getting that ball to the hole through proper speed and feel. Susan thus had a great sense of how to hit the ball and most beginners don't ever get that sense of how hard or soft to hit the ball with the putter.

As long as you can get the right speed, you can then advance and figure out breaks and slope and all of the intricate stuff. Most people who begin to play golf lose that concept of speed and then the rest is downhill.

The other aspect of putting is practice. People need to practice those three-footers and four-footers and five-footers. Those simple putts need to become routine. All too often the players say, "That's a gimme!" No. I don't agree. There are no gimmes on the tour.

How would you like to never three-putt again? The way to do this is to spend a lot of time practicing those three- and four-foot putts. After you know you can make these, just work on your lag putting. If you can lag it within three feet, then there go those three-putts.

I am one of five people to have the lowest number of putts in a round in a PGA tour event: eighteen. It only took me one putt a green for eighteen holes to get that ball in the hole.

I'm not expecting myself or anyone else to go out there and play that way all the time. I'm just saying that if a golfer practices his or her putts from that critical five-foot distance, the game will be so much friendlier in the end on that person's scorecard.

PLUMB BOBBING

Many times on television the viewer will see the professionals hold their putter up in the air in a vertical position and look through the putter. You probably wonder what they're doing. They're plumb bobbing. This is the same thing that a mason will do to make sure that a structure is level. The golfers are merely using this technique to read the putts.

I don't use this technique. I'm not good at applying it, and the technique is not helpful to me. It's most useful in golf courses in the mountains because of many elevation changes. You can misread a green with regard to breaks and slopes, but if your speed is good, your position will be better than the golfer who reads the green perfectly and putts the ball so that it lips the hole and goes twelve feet downhill the wrong way.

If you want to be a plumb bobber, here's how it's done. You need to do some simple things before even employing the technique. First, figure out which eye is your dominant eye. You pick a spot on the wall in front of you. You look at it with both eyes open. Close your left eye first. Then close your right eye. If you close your right eye and the spot doesn't move, then your left eye is dominant, and vice versa. Now you have your dominant eye. You're ready to take out that putter.

Stand behind the ball. Take the putter and hang it in midair with one hand and place the putter so that the bottom is over ball. Line up the hole and the ball using your dominant eye. Now you will know which way the green breaks. You've created a perfectly straight line, and by doing so you can now see the tilt of the green.

Speed, however, is still the X factor in my book. The plumb bobber still doesn't know the most critical aspect of putting using this technique, and that's the speed of the green. Speed comes from feeling the firmness of the green, from looking at the green and seeing how close to the ground the grass is and how the balls from other players have been playing that day.

Plumb bobbing is a good technique for judging the tilt of the green, but you'll still need to have depth perception for judging the little knolls that might run through the green head-on, and you'll still need to judge the speed, or X factor, for yourself.

If you can use this method effectively, then do it. I've been on tour these many years and it is not my method of choice. I feel more comfortable walking on the green and judging its slope by eyeballing it. That's what works best for me.

16. The Best Putters

All of the greatest golfers are great putters. Some just took great putting to an exceptional level. Jack Nicklaus made every putt. Arnold Palmer was fantastic as well, and Tom Watson and Billy Casper made some unbelievable putts in some clutch situations.

However, Bob Charles was one of the first players who was all arms and shoulders when he putted. He kept his back straight and remained straight throughout the putting stroke.

Ben Crenshaw was an equally terrific putter with a totally different style of putting. He was an imaginative putter. He was what we call on the tour a feel-and-touch putter. No matter where he was on the green he'd putt the ball within a foot of the hole.

In my opinion we've had a great many players who were great putters because it's rather hard to remain successful on the PGA TOUR if you're not a fantastic putter. Although there are putting rankings, everyone is still phenomenal. They're just comparing phenomenal with superhuman.

The best thinker from my days on the tour would be Tom Watson. Like Jack, he was in complete control of his game and remained focused.

Dave Stockton always had a great attitude, and he accomplished a lot because of his mental toughness. He was another marvelous putter.

However, the award for the two classic putting moments in recent years should be handed to Nick Faldo and Doug Sanders, but for opposite reasons.

Nick Faldo won the Masters in 1990 with a spectacular putt at the eleventh hole in a playoff along the way, and he threw his club up in the air and almost killed himself. Doug Sanders had to make a two-foot putt to win the British Open. He missed the putt and lost the British Open to Nicklaus in what is one of the most heartbreaking major losses.

Brad Faxon is also a great putter. What makes him so good is that he has this nice stroke and setup. His routine enables him to putt the same way all the time, and he believes he can make every putt. This mental aspect is so important to golf. There are many players on tour who have the ability to make great putts, but they don't believe in themselves, and so they fail. Brad is more of an arms-and-shoulders-type putter.

Fuzzy Zoeller made a long putt at the eleventh hole to win the Masters in the playoffs and the tragic aspect to the story is how he made it into the playoffs. He only got into the playoffs because Ed Sneed missed three short putts in the last three holes that were about five feet from the hole each time. Who knows what would have happened to Ed Sneed's career had he made one of those putts and had won the Masters.

17. My Advice on Putting

When you finally get to the tour level, you've already worked through many of the physical and mental aspects of the game. When you have to make a putt that means something, that's where your background becomes important. By background I mean the time spent on the putting green developing a muscle memory, whereby your body recognizes what feels right and what feels comfortable. You have already developed a "stroke," and now it's up to you to execute that stroke, focusing on the line of the putt and the speed of the green. You have to visualize the ball going into the hole and then stand over the ball, go through your routine, and make the putt. It sounds simple enough, but it's not simple at all. For that brief thirty seconds in time, the success or failure of your putt attempt will be dictated by the thousands of hours you've spent on the practice greens over the years.

When people come up to me and ask me about "putts under pressure," in my mind there can be no bigger putt than the putt made by the late Payne Stewart in 1999 to win the U.S. Open. Payne made a fifteen-foot putt on the last hole to win the U.S. Open. He knocked that putt down right in the middle of the hole. It was the longest putt made on the last hole of the U.S. Open to win by one shot.

It is this mental toughness which many golfers across the country can develop and thus help make them better golfers, and golfers who enjoy the game a lot more! Remember, you have to go out and enjoy the game. Great putters have great mechanics as a prerequisite, but what distinguishes one great golfer from another is his mental toughness. You can line up everyone on the entire tour and they would all have great mechanics. However, it is the fine line of mental toughness that distinguishes the great ones. The select few aren't going to give in to missing that putt. They're going to make it, plain and simple.

How does someone pick a putting style? Putting is as individualistic as any facet of the game of golf. Some players putt with their bodies aimed toward the right, some are aimed toward the left, but the key to putting, as to the rest of golf, is muscle memory. You want to keep the putter squared to the line back and forth, but stance, grip, and posture are very individual. You need to go to the putting green and see what feels comfortable. Many tour players change stance and grip right in the middle of a round! They see that on that particular day things aren't going well, so they readjust their position until their body feels comfortable.

I stumbled onto the style I used by fiddling around on the practice green. Lee Milligan was my mentor, but nobody gave me a putting style. You can't give someone a style. They need to find their own style. I developed my putting style in college because as I practiced putting more and more, I just went with what felt comfortable to me. Then Lee and I would work on things around that style. Coaches can work with you on your style, but you need to find out what works best for you. The formal lessons gave me the following: the idea of lining myself up "square to the line" and remaining "equally balanced between both feet" and that the head of the putter needed to flow back straight away from the ball and then straight through the ball, keeping everything very square. Within these precepts I fiddled around with different grips, different stances (wider stances, narrower stances), but I always stayed pretty square to the line.

Golfers (beginners or advanced) need to experiment and see what works best for them. The tour players have all experimented. The difference between a good putter and an average putter on tour is making one more putt a day!

Some players have gone to a cross-handed style of putting. By cross-handed I mean exchanging hands, whereby you place your left hand low on the grip (if you're a right-handed putter) and your right hand high, instead of the usual right hand low, left hand high. It's a great technique. Many more people should try this grip! It helps a player to keep from breaking down at impact. Breaking down occurs when your wrists cave in and the putter head goes ahead of your hands. If you are a person who breaks down at contact, the left-hand-low method would be very good for you as a way of correcting the problem. You would be forced to keep your hands and forearms moving toward the target without breaking down.

I'll give you two vastly different styles of putting, but both have the same result of success. There's the "old school" and the "new school." Let's look at Billy Casper. Billy Casper was one of the great players of our time, and he was a fabulous putter. He doesn't get anywhere near the recognition that he should, and he's won majors and tournaments galore. To be exact, in fact, Billy Casper is sixth on the all-time tour win list. He has fifty-one tour wins! Only Sam Snead, Jack Nicklaus, Ben Hogan, Arnold Palmer, and Byron Nelson have more tour wins than Casper!

Billy Casper used what would be considered a pop stroke. This was a stroke many players used before 1970 because the greens were slow. The stroke required a tremendous amount of hand usage and movement in hands and wrist to pop the ball.

Modern-day players use more arms and shoulders and not much hands. Ben Crenshaw and Bob Charles, Brad Faxon, Payne Stewart, use this new approach, whereby the V created between your shoulders and hands (the triangle) swung the putter. This is a great technique today because the greens have become so much faster. Tiger Woods uses this stroke today, and he's a phenomenal putter. This is the kind of stroke I've always tried to use (and I used this method when I won my two U.S. Open Championships), whereby I was using my arms and shoulders and not any "hands" at all. Bob Charles, one of the greatest left-handers, should be credited as the first to really perfect this style of putting, however.

Most PGA TOUR players use putters that are between 34 inches and 36 inches long. Lee Jansen uses a slightly shorter putter. I've used a 35-inch putter over the years, but I choke up on it a lot. It's the "choking" up on the club that made the club appear so much shorter than it was.

Again, whether you're old school or new school, the result should be the same: making the putt when it counts. My recommendation is to use the arms-and-shoulders method, and try the cross-handed grip. It just might be the surprise of your golfing life!

18. Let Me Help Your Game!

Maybe you know the game of golf, but you struggle when your lie is poor or when you're in the rough. I can help you. Trust me. What follows are the most common problems encountered on the golf course and how to solve them easily and save your score in the process. I have given many corporate clinics and have instructed all of my partners in the corporate outings in the same manner. Even when I played in ProAms with avid golfers these problems surfaced, and my answer to these men and women, whether they be entertainers, authors, musicians, or corporate heads, is always the same. There are a few situations in golf where the advice I give never changes.

Problem One—You've just hit a tee shot and the ball lands right in the heart of the fairway. You stroll to your beautiful shot two-hundred-plus yards away only to want to cry. There is a nice divot in the fairway and your tee shot has found that divot. There is plenty of beautiful fairway all around you, but your ball has been magnetically drawn, or so it seems, to that divot. Don't panic. The first thing people think about when they arrive at their ball only to see it in a divot is, "How can I lift my ball out of that divot?" Don't try to do this ever. My theory has always been to hit down on the ball really squarely and solidly, instead of trying to scoop it out of that divot. Take out a club that is one number lower than what you would normally use in that situation and position yourself so that the ball is ever so slightly closer to your right foot. As an example, take a five- instead of a six-iron. Choke up on the club and hit down into the ball, as if you wanted to drive it into the ground. What that does is enable the natural loft of the club face to take over, and the club does all the work. The club face lifts the ball out of the divot. Hit down into the ball. Don't scoop it, or else the ball will be hit "fat" or will be topped, and it will just roll down the fairway another twenty or thirty yards.

It's amazing how many good shots you can hit out of divots if you just don't get upset. That's the other factor: your temperament. Many times when you walk to that ball and see that it has found that divot, you're mad. Try not to get mad. Keep your composure. Understand that a great shot is still possible.

Problem Two—Let's say your tee shot lands off the fairway, but in that first cut of rough. This is called the "intermediate rough" and you can usually hit your normal club, and even a club with a higher number. Yes, I said a higher-numbered club in some cases. In other words, the light rough is not going to hurt you at all, especially if the ball is sitting on top of the blades of grass. This shot is one that can become a "flyer." A "flyer" in golf is a ball that is positioned such that blades of grass are embedded between the ball and the club face at the point of contact. The effect of the embedded grass is that of a knuckleball reaction. Just as in baseball, if you throw a ball without any spin, the ball can dance and go anywhere and it's almost unhittable. In golf the principle is the same when it comes to the flyer.

Just remember that when you have a flyer lie, the ball won't stop as quickly when it hits the green, and because of this you can use a shorter club for your approach.

Problem Three—What happens if your tee shot goes into the deep rough? Now you arrive at your ball and you find it buried at the bottom of that deep junk. What do you do? Let's say you're 180 yards from the green and the club you'd normally use in that situation is a five-wood. Don't use that five wood here because the rough is too deep to use that club effectively. This is where, through practice, you learn which club you can hit to make that ball go the farthest out of that rough. Sometimes you can get away using an eight-iron. The whole key is not hitting the club based on book yardage. Forget the yardage-club rule you normally employ. The rough is so thick in these situations that the key to the whole strategy is getting that ball back into play on the fairway. Often a golfer will be able to hit the ball farther using a nine-iron than he or she will using their normal six-iron in that situation. Experimenting is the key. Practice beforehand in deep rough or in a situation that simulates deep rough, such as uncut lawn grass. This way, when the situation arises in a round of golf you will be able to execute your strategy effectively. Loft is the key here. You need a club with a lot of loft.

Problem Four—The ball is hit into the woods and there is a nice, big, beautiful tree right in front of you! Now what do you do, besides cry? You just get out of the situation and save par in the process. Sounds easier said than done. It's easy to do, and I'll walk you through it. The problem here may seem at first to be the lie of the ball. It's not as if you're in deep rough. The trees tend to have barren patches around you because the trees shade the areas immediately underneath them. In actuality, the lie here is better than you thought if you know how to approach the shot.

Someone once wrote an article explaining that "trees are 80 percent air." That's the stupidest thing I've ever heard in my entire life! "Just hit it up through the trees. It's just nothing but leaves up there!" Yeah, until it clanks a tree limb and the ball falls down right beside you after an ear-deafening embarrassing "knock" made by your ball hitting that big branch up near the top of the tree. People, believing in that article, have probably tried it again and again, only to hear "knock, knock." Two more shots. Two more balls returned to you by Mr. Tree!

You need to figure out how to get the ball back into play and not be concerned about how far you are from the hole or whether you're shot is perfectly clear. Most average players, if they were to pitch the ball back into the fairway, would have a lower score for that hole than if they "went for it" with the big blast. Everyone wants to go for it. People think that if they just blast it out from behind that tree or from between the trees, the ball will soar into the air, over the branches, and onto the green. What usually happens is that the ball comes flying back in their face or lands right by their feet in the original position, and they make an eight on that hole. The smart player chips out and gets a clean fairway lie.

The experienced player can try their hand at a hook shot or a slice shot. These techniques allow you to hit the ball onto the fairway, but farther up toward the hole. Now you might be able to slice the ball and run the ball up almost onto the green or hook the ball onto the green.

If you want to "slice" the ball here's how it's done. I recommend practicing this technique. First you need to establish the position for a perfectly straight shot. Draw two imaginary lines in front of you, as if you were making railroad tracks. Place your feet, hips, and shoulders all parallel with that lower line. The other line is used as a guide to make sure the club face is square to the ball and aimed at the target. To fade the shot, or slice the shot, keep the club face square with the ball and with the line, but move the other line. Aim the bottom line to the left. Your feet, hips, and shoulders are now aimed to the left. As you take your backswing, the swing will come around outside the line of intended flight, and as it comes back through the ball it cuts across the ball from outside inward, which will cause the ball to have left-to-right spin on it and make it fade, or "slice." The principle is to change the position of one of the units out of the two-unit system. Change your feet-hands-hip-shoulder unit. Keep the club face–ball-aim unit the same.

In the game of baseball if you want, as a right-handed hitter, to hit the ball to right field, then you wait back on the ball and it will spray toward right field. In golf, you are changing the position of that feet-hips-shoulder unit while keeping your swing and club face positioned as it was before, changing nothing within that unit. Because the club face is still aimed at the target, it will make the ball spin from left to right.

For a hook shot, go back to the original position of keeping everything in line with those two imaginary railroad tracks. Now, move the bottom line consisting of your feet, hips, and shoulders to the right. Keep the top line, or unit consisting of the club face, ball, and your aim, the same. Now, the intended line of flight will be changed so that the ball hooks.

The principle is simple. Now just apply it. The tree can be "gotten around" now, and your life is not so complicated. Trees may be 80 percent air by volume, but their cross-sectional opening to the flight of the ball is only 5 percent.

Problem Five—You've hit the ball well outside of the fairway, and now it's situated underneath some low-to-the-ground sprawling bush or underneath a very small tree. This is a hard shot. If you take a backswing and your club hits the limbs of the tree and leaves fall out of the tree or out of the bush, then technically you've improved your lie according to the USGA rules, and it just cost you at least one stroke. In this case practicing far back from the shot is better, and when you make the shot you might want to consider taking a half swing. The little swings can make the ball jump out and back onto the fairway. Don't try and do too much here. If the 25-handicapper would just try to get these specific types of shots back in play, they would save ten shots a round. Think about how many times you played and you felt in your heart that you played well, but your scorecard doesn't reflect it. It's usually because of a few bad holes. My advice is to play a head game with yourself and tell yourself that par just went up one stroke at this hole. Mentally what this does for you is it allows you to get that ball out of trouble and onto the fairway and you can make par or bogey at worst. Accept a 5 on this par-4 hole, and your overall score will be lower.

Problem Six—The ball goes off the green a bit too far, and suddenly you're on the collar of that deep greenside rough. No problem. Use a sand wedge and top the ball purposely "blading" it. The sharp edge of the sand wedge cuts through the grass if some blades are abutting the ball, whereas the putter will have an uneven follow-through because of the blades of grass interfering with the head of the putter. Sometimes a player will use a fairway wood as a putter when the ball enters the deeper greenside rough, beyond the normal low-cut fringe. The fairway wood has just enough loft to the club face that the club face allows the ball to hop over the first foot or two of grass, and the ball rolls along like a putt. Most amateurs just need to practice these shots at the putting green.

Problem Seven—Your head. Sometimes games get derailed not because of bad shots but because of bad thoughts. Generally most players will do better the less they beat themselves up over the course of a round. Many times when one thing goes wrong a player will collapse for four or five holes before they return to normalcy. That's too long to take to regroup. You should never let anything get to you on the golf course for that long. Think about it. Five holes is slightly less than one-third of the course. This means you're angry or off kilter for more than 30 percent of the time you're out there. Don't do that to yourself. It's amazing how many times during the course of a round where you make a good decision (i.e., to get the ball back into play instead of going for the green) that you hit your normal fairway wedge shot and the ball goes onto the green and rolls five feet from the hole. It's almost as if the proverbial Golf Gods are smiling at you because you made a smart decision instead of a stupid one.

Part Three

Golf's Senior Personalities

There would never have been a need for a golf book if these legends hadn't decided to play golf.

19. The King

I think all of us as professional golfers owe a huge amount of gratitude to Arnold Palmer. There have been many great players, and legends of the game—Jack Nicklaus, Gary Player—just to name two of the greatest ever. Arnold Palmer, however, arrived on the golf scene and really made the game of golf much of what it is today. He brought golf to the forefront in popular culture and he brought it into the homes of millions on national television.

Arnold Palmer is a man of few words but much action. His actions always speak louder than his words. I think one of his best legacies in golf is his deep love of the game. He showed me how to be a professional golfer from a public relations standpoint. He would sign autographs for hours after a given round of golf, and it showed me that I had an obligation to the fans.

He also has a sense of family values, and his thoughts about family and fatherhood, which he privately shared with me, made a lasting impression on me as to how to conduct my life.

Arnold took great pleasure in going out and playing practice rounds with some of the younger players just to check them out. Can you imagine what it felt like for me to be twenty-two, new on tour, to have Arnold playing beside me?

I remember the fall of 1972. I missed qualifying at Hilton Head, which was the next to last tournament of the year. I qualified and made the cut at the Walt Disney Classic, the last tournament of the year. This was one of the most important things that happened to me as a professional golfer because by making the cut at Disney, it got me into the Los Angeles Open the next year. This was the first tournament of the 1973 golf calendar. Back then if you made the cut on the last tournament of the year, you were automatically in the next tournament. At the start of the year there would be two or three hundred players on Monday qualifying for three or four or five slots. For me, knowing that I was going to be in the Los Angeles Open was a huge confidence builder. I thought that if I could be productive at the Los Angeles Open, good things would be right around the corner for me.

Here's how my first Arnold encounter started. The 1973 calendar year was my first full year, my rookie year. There I was, playing in the L.A. Open at Riviera Country Club. The club itself is a landmark, dating back to 1927. When you play there you feel a sense of history. On a personal note, I was starting a new life for myself now then— both in golf and with my wife. Susan and I had been married for six months, and we were just two kids starting off our marriage feeling that we were two of the luckiest people in the world.

In my first round I struggled. I was lucky to shoot 75. I came back on Friday to shoot 70 and make the cut. What a great start.

Although I was thrilled to make the cut, because it enabled me to play the next week in the Phoenix Open, I never thought I'd be paired alongside the legendary Arnold Palmer. Immediately after seeing the pairing sheets I picked up the hotel telephone and called to recheck to make sure this was true. I didn't sleep at all that night.

I got to the third hole and hit a beautiful approach shot that landed three feet from the cup. No one clapped for me. Arnold hit the ball thirty feet from the hole and they went crazy, cheering him on,

"Arnold, Arnold!" That was to be expected because I was the kid and he was the King.

When we arrived at the fourth hole, I had honors. The fourth hole is a 240-yard par-3. There I was, at twenty-two years of age, and I took out my one-iron from my bag and I hit this beautiful shot. The ball flew through the air the way you dreamed it would, and it landed right in the heart of the green. Arnold at the time had his longtime caddie, Creamy, with him.

Creamy was a great caddie, and Arnold looked at him and said, "Creamy, do you think this is a two or a three?" Creamy looked at him and, after having seen me hit this one-iron that I absolutely crushed, said, "Arnold, you don't carry a two-wood."

I was shocked that anybody would say anything like that to Arnold Palmer. Arnold got a little ruffled and he grabbed his three-iron and put the ball in the front bunker. It was true, pure Arnold. It was fantastic. We walked off the tee laughing about it. He said, "You hit that pretty hard, didn't you?" I sheepishly grinned and thanked him.

I was playing at the TPC shortly after my first U.S. Open victory. I happened to be paired with Arnold Palmer and Jack Nicklaus. The voice over the microphone introduced Arnold. "Four-time Masters champion, U.S. Open champion, sixty wins." He teed off. Then came the introduction for Jack. "Four-time Masters champion, four-time U.S. Open champion, six-time PGA champion, PGA Player of the Year." He teed off. Then came me. I never felt so insignificant in all my life after hearing those introductions. What could they say about me? I had won a U.S. Open, but I felt as if I was their tagalong for the day.

Arnold Palmer set a standard for golf that was high not only from a playing standpoint but also from a human standpoint. The gusto and sheer joy that he had while playing was what made him the King. When I think of sleepless nights, I think of that day I found out that

I was paired with Arnold Palmer, and then I reflect on how nicely he treated me the next day. He is a real person. He has kingly status but is a regular person at the same time with respect to how he treats people. He is an icon of American popular culture, and he changed the way people looked at our sport in the 1960s. He brought sport to television.

When Arnold was diagnosed with prostate cancer, I was saddened. He knew he would be back and could beat the cancer. His cancer slapped me in the face because here's someone whom I had idolized as a child and now called friend, and he was ill. The first thing I did when I found out was call him and ask if there was anything my family could do to help. The thoughts were running through my head, "How could Arnold get this? He shouldn't be sick. He shouldn't have anything wrong with him." I knew, however, that this was just another bump in the road and that he would beat it, and he did!

Arnold Palmer proved himself to be a hero in the medical world, as he *wanted* to do something to further research for prostate cancer so that others afflicted by the disease could be cured. He made men aware of the importance of checking the PSA count and seeing their internists for regular checkups. I thought to myself, "If it could happen to Arnold Palmer, it could certainly happen to me." I would suspect that all of us went and had our PSAs checked within a month of learning about Arnold contracting the disease.

Arnold is still a down-to-earth person to this day, and he plays golf with a bunch of regular guys every single day at Bay Hill. It's unbelievable that his attitude has not changed since 1955. He's more than 70 years old, and he acts like a young thirty-year-old, and he has as many commercials and advertisements as anyone in sports—and for good reason. He's believable. He's honorable. He stands for something. You can't say that about a lot of athletes today.

Arnold was the perfect guy at the perfect time and was the original swing-from-your-heels golfer. He changed golf as dramatically in the

1950s and 1960s as Tiger Woods is doing in the 2000s. He got the entire steel mill areas of Pittsburgh to care about golf. He was strong and he'd swing mightily and his shirt would come out. He'd lose his balance he swung so hard at times. Television was tailor-made for Arnold. He influenced an earlier generation in much the same way as Michael Jordan has affected today's youth. MJ has done more for basketball than anyone in bringing the game to the entire world. Michael brought basketball to the international scene, and Arnold made golf an internationally marketed sport. It all started when Arnold went overseas and tore up the British Open. When Arnold won the British Open, the story made headlines everywhere. Suddenly the British Open was a tournament with a media gallery. The event needed all the coverage it could get, as it had first reached full worldwide news coverage only within the previous fifteen years.

Just a few years back when I was broadcasting for Home Depot in Charlotte on the SENIOR PGA TOUR, I got to see the vintage Arnold in full form and fashion. He played a great round on Friday, and I was out covering him with his group on Saturday for ESPN. He was probably four shots out of the lead and was a realistic contender at this time. He shot this magnificent 69 on Friday and was about to shoot the same, or 70, on Saturday. Suddenly he hit this great drive on the eighteenth hole.

The eighteenth green is kind of a peninsula stuck out in the water. There's not a great percentage in your favor to hit the green on your second shot. Arnold was 250 yards out. I thought this was going to be a conservative shot and was waiting for him to take out his iron when suddenly he amazed me. He took out this wood! A wood! On national television on Saturday when everyone was watching I said, "What's he doing?" This was before he even hit the shot. I thought he was nuts. It was a shot a person could not pull off more than once in ten tries! It was crazy.

My thinking was that he should lay up, then knock it onto the green with a wedge; this would have given him a good birdie opportunity. He could have finished the day on a positive note and could have finished in the top 3 starting on Sunday. Instead, he hit the ball right smack into the water and ended up his chances for a birdie.

I walked over to him. "What were you doing??" I asked him in an exasperated tone. He turned to me and said, "Andy, all these people waiting on the last hole came to see Arnold Palmer and I gave them Arnold Palmer! I went for the green!" That's Arnold in a nutshell! If the people wanted it, he'd try it to make *them* happy. He wanted to please his fans. Nobody has felt more of an obligation to their fans than Arnold Palmer. I think it's really admirable that he has always felt this way. It's crazy, but it's cool.

Over the years we've become great friends and we have played a lot of golf together. Just being around him is one of the greatest experiences for me. Playing with Arnold Palmer is a thrill. The crowd is vociferously on his side, and this just makes me want to play even better and raise my game to another level.

20. "Iron" Byron Nelson

Byron Nelson was the man who once shared with me some words of golfing wisdom I'll never forget. "To be a great golfer," he said, "you have to be either brilliant or brain dead, and anybody in the middle has a lot of trouble!"

I think it's true. If you don't think too much about the ninety-nine things that could go wrong with your swing, then you'll play well. Who would have thought that the fifteen-year-old Nelson, who on December 23, 1927, met fellow fifteen-year-old prodigy Ben Hogan in a playoff for the Glen Garden Country Club caddie championship in Fort Worth, would have gone on to be the legendary golfer with the historic streak. That day in 1927 belonged to young Nelson as he beat Hogan by one stroke.

Nelson was intuitive, and given his wisdom, I would say he was brilliant. His shot selection and his knack for mastering the mental aspects of the game of golf were far superior to anyone. Just as we all have personal sides to us in addition to professional aspects of our lives, Byron was just as great off the course as he was on the course.

Byron Nelson is truly one of the great gentlemen of golf. I was fortunate enough to meet Mr. Nelson through Tom Watson. He helped

Tom tremendously with his game, and Tom and I played quite a number of practice rounds together. Every once in a while Mr. Nelson would walk around with us. One of the neatest aspects of Byron's personality was that he always made you feel as if you were important. He just treated people so nicely. He was one of those very rare people who didn't speak about himself, but rather he let others talk about him. What he accomplished in our game was so incredible and yet he never told anyone about it. He never sat around over lunch talking about what he accomplished at this course and at that course.

On a personal note, one of my fondest memories of Byron was when Tom Watson and I were playing a practice round at Augusta one year. The great Byron Nelson was out there in the fresh Georgia air walking around with us. It was early in the morning and there weren't a lot of people out on the course. It felt as if we had Iron Byron to ourselves.

Tom and I were on the back nine and we kept asking Byron if he wanted to hit a shot. We knew he would take us up on our offer eventually, although we didn't know how long it would take him to surrender to temptation. As we expected, he just kept saying that he didn't want to hit.

Finally, as the holes dwindled, he succumbed. Not only did he swing the club, but he ended up playing some holes with us! Here was a man who hadn't played in years and he played four holes with us that day. He played a shot that day I'll never forget at the fourteenth hole. He drove the ball up on top of the big hill, played a four-iron from that point, and ran the ball up that big slope. The outcome was the ball ended up running and running and stopped about two feet from the hole. The people out there with us just went crazy and we were laughing and having a great time.

When we were finished playing that day, Byron invited us to lunch. I sat around the table, alongside my dad, talking golf with the great

Byron Nelson. It was one of the great days in my golfing life because we actually got Byron to talk about that magical year of 1945 when he won all of those tournaments in that terrific streak.

Just thinking about that year, I myself can't imagine that many victories in a row. He won the 1945 PGA Championship at the Moraine Country Club in Dayton, Ohio, beating Sam Byrd. He won at the Tam O'Shanter All-American for a tenth victory in a row. He won his eleventh tournament in a row on August fourth of that year, winning at the Canadian Open.

What amazed me most about Mr. Nelson that day at lunch was how he addressed that magical year. Byron spoke about how well he was playing but also about how lucky he was during the streak. He never bragged. In fact it was quite the opposite. It was actually like pulling teeth to get him to tell that story. I felt more like a dentist than a golfer.

The whole point of his victorious season was that if he needed to shoot 63 or 64 to win, he'd find a way to do it. His scoring average that year was ridiculously low, and his scoring average on Sundays for the year was in the mid-60s!

Shortly after our conversation he wrote a little black book about that year, and it was fantastic. I have often thought about how beautiful that diary was.

I've spoken to many golfers who have played the game for many years and they're always comparing the current generation to the older generation. That is not so when it comes to Byron Nelson. Byron's very up-front with everyone. He talks about how good these players of today are, and he won't let anyone take anything away from the modern-day players. He is truly one of the great promoters of golf because he has a great personality and a lot of legend to his name. He retired at his prime. Not many golfers can say that about themselves. He just wanted to do something else and has done a lot of wonderful things.

He's done television, written books, built golf courses, and he's truly a gifted woodworker.

I think Byron's truly one of the nicest human beings that I've ever met.

21. Gene Sarazen

Let's talk about Gene Sarazen as the ultimate equipment guru. In 1932, Gene Sarazen won his second U.S. Open and his first British Open. Thanks to Mr. Sarazen, the world was treated to the sand wedge, and we as a golfing group became rather intrigued by the manufacturing of golf clubs. Gene Sarazen's genuine love of all aspects of the game of golf led to him developing new clubs and new standards for club manufacturers.

I first met Gene Sarazen at the age of sixteen, when I happened to be touring the Wilson factory and he happened to be at the factory that day. I was introduced to him and he, in turn, introduced me to the side of golf I had never seen. He took me with him inside the Wilson manufacturing plant and told me all about the making of golf clubs.

I just couldn't believe it was all happening to me. He was a man packed full of energy and excitement and his enthusiasm was contagious. Even in his nineties he had a love for the game and loved to talk about the game. He's the kind of guy who would talk all day long about a particular golf club. More important, he was the type of guy who could not only speak to you about a sand wedge or a particular club, but by the conversation's end you couldn't wait to tour a factory where sand wedges were made or where irons were made. I was bitten by the club-manufacturing bug as a result of my meeting him that day.

What I learned that day with him at the Wilson plant was incredible. I was the proverbial kid in the candy shop. I had owned only a few sets of clubs in my life, and now I was around bins and bins of drivers, putters, and sand wedges, with a man who loved the making of them all.

Touring the factory showed me all about the making of the golf club, in particular how club faces were bent and shaped and how all of this affected the flight of the ball. The shafts, halves, and grips must all be in harmony with each other. Shafts were tested to see whether they were all the same. The makers weighed the shafts in front of me, then placed them on a "deflection board," as they called it. By placing the shafts on the board, the makers were able to determine how pronounced the bend was to each shaft. The golfer needed to know this information so that all of his shafts were matched up, because if they weren't all matched up there would be an inconsistency of flex in the club. If there was such an inconsistency, then the result of a struck ball might be an errant flight. The swing weights needed to be the same as well. It was fun to see all of this happening before my eyes, but it was extra special to me because I was experiencing it with the great Gene Sarazen.

Gene was the first player to understand that it would be easier to get the ball out of the deep bunkers by using a club with a lot of loft and one that would enable the golfer get that bounce necessary to get out of the greenside bunkers cleanly. He knew that if a flange was added to the bottom of the highest lofted club, the club would work better and would produce a uniform result out of the bunker. Gene pressed forward and developed his sand wedge, and that is why today we are able to get out of the sand with effortless ease.

Today this principle is taken for granted, but when Gene voiced these ideas it went against the grain. The golf world was lagging behind Gene when it came to golf strategy. When we as professionals give clinics and teach about the importance of having in your golf bag a club that is specifically for bunker play and is both comfortable and has great loft, we should be thanking Gene Sarazen for showing us the light of day.

22. Sam Snead

Sam Snead was probably the best ever at messing up other players. He was an expert at getting inside your head if you dared look too suspiciously at him. In baseball it would be analogous to a catcher playing games with a batter where he knows the batter is stealing signs off him.

If Sam ever caught a young player looking in his bag to judge what club he should be hitting, Sam would get up on that hole and make a big swing and hit this soft shot right on the green, and then he'd show his club. This was the beginning of the end for the nosy young golfer. The other golfer would end up using the same club and would swing the club using his normal stroke for that particular club, and all of a sudden things went downhill quickly. That kid would end up hitting the ball over the green and would be standing there puzzled. We called this "bag hawking" on the tour. If Sam caught you bag hawking, watch out! He had this unbelievable ability to make a variety of shots with the same club with what, again, looked like the same swing.

In actuality he had such pinpoint muscle memory and control that he could take any club and, by controlling the amount of pressure he put into a specific swing, hit the ball where he desired. The most amazing thing about his demonstrations were that he could use a five-iron from close range and get the ball to go right to the cup, and he could make you think he took his natural "hard" five-iron swing! If you copied him, the ball would fly miles over the green. He had that God-given gift of being able to train his muscles to maintain rhythm throughout.

I played quite a few practice rounds with Sam Snead, and I loved to watch him hit golf balls. I was paired with him a few times. He was the greatest that I've ever seen at being able to take a particular club out of his bag and hit the ball a variety of distances with what looked like the same swing. He could take a five-iron and hit it 150 yards or 185 yards and his swing didn't look any different. He and Byron Nelson had some terrific matches during their time, and it's been great to see both of them teeing off at the majors.

One of the important things he would mention to me as we practiced together was that the golf swing had to be constant motion. He had this beautiful waggle that started his golf swing. To him, this was very important. We talked about that a lot and how to keep the club moving. Very few good players start from the stopped position. They always manage to keep the club moving. He was probably the best at this, and he had wonderful rhythm and balance in his golf swing. Arguably he's one of the best two or three players to ever play the game.

23. Charlie Sifford

Charlie Sifford is a pioneer in this game of golf, breaking racial barriers. He was the Jackie Robinson of professional golf and he was one of the men I admire most in the game. I have had the privilege of golfing with Charlie many times, and every time I played with him I would make these fantastic putts. I made putts from everywhere. He called me "One-Putt" for thirty years. Charlie is himself "Mr. One-Putt" because he could always get the ball into the hole.

Here is a man who went through more than anybody could ever go through, and he still has a positive attitude and he's always friendly. Charlie played the game at the highest level for many, many years and still can hit it with the best of them. He loves to smoke his cigar and tell stories and compete. Charlie truly loved being around the players.

The hardships for Charlie hadn't ended even by the time I turned professional. When Charlie and I were playing at Greensboro, hecklers yelled every racial epithet at him and even threw beer cans at him, and therefore me, on the green. That day I looked around and I couldn't believe how he could endure this, and how he endured what he went through for years before my time. It was horrible. I myself would not have been able to go through thirty years of that type of physical and verbal abuse. Charlie had an inner strength second to none. He was going to live out his childhood dreams and play golf and be one of the greatest no matter what happened. Golf at that time was a country club sport in the worst sense of the word. The golfers who were in the game were living in a racially closed vacuum. Charlie had to break those barriers, and being a pioneer often involves taking abuse and not receiving one's fair share in life. At that time in society things weren't fair. That Charlie overcame what he did and that he was able to smile at his peers and at the world speaks volumes for him as a person.

Charlie and I would talk about golf and golf strategy. The Mutual Legends of Golf is great because I get to hear guys like Charlie talk golf: golf strategy and golf memories. I watched Charlie, and I took away a lot from him. From watching him, I learned how to compete to the very end. He was creative with the game and always made the shot he needed to make. He was a smart player. He would make the conservative shot when the situation called for it, and he went for the tough shot when the situation called for that. He knew how to win.

My biggest regret was that our careers didn't overlap much. I did play with him at practice rounds, but not the hundreds of times I wish I'd have played with him. However, having done ESPN television on the SENIOR PGA TOUR I saw him make some unbelievable shots. He has a great sense of humor as well, and he loves to joke around with people. He loves that back-and-forth banter of good friendship. It was only later on in his career that the media and the golfing world really appreciated him.

Sometimes it's hard for us to realize the greatness in people until it's too late. I hope Charlie understands the respect and admiration that his peers have for him.

24. Tommy Bolt and Tom Weiskopf

Every so often a sport experiences a flamboyant player with style and vigor, and the skills to take them to the promised land. Such was the case for "Terrible" Tommy Bolt. Bolt took golf by storm, both on and off the course. He is classy and comical and is never at a loss for the flamboyant display of emotion.

Tommy Bolt was the first touring professional golfer I ever saw play. I was in high school at the time, and our golf team had a excursion to the 1964 Western Open. We ventured out to the Tam O'Shanter Country Club in Illinois. I was a young, impressionable kid, and I couldn't wait to finally see a real live professional up close. This was exciting to me because at night I sometimes dreamed about being a professional golfer.

There he was, the great Tommy Bolt on a par-5 hole. He took his swing and he hit his second shot. The ball ended up hitting a tree, then ricocheting into the woods. I saw Tommy get mad and the next thing we all knew he quit! I saw him just walk off the course. It was amazing. My first thoughts were how serious this guy must be about his golf game and how much he must care to just walk off after hitting a tree. That was my introduction to the great Tommy Bolt.

Tommy was, and still is, an immaculate dresser. It might seem insignificant to the person who doesn't know Tommy, but Tommy will read this and know I'm giving him the utmost compliment. Players sometimes say they don't care how they look, but Tommy always cared, and he cares to this very day. He wore the best slacks, the best shirts, and the best shoes. He wore the classiest sweaters and had the pants with the creases that made you ooh and aah when you looked at him.

He is a stylish and dapper guy to this day, whether it be in a car or on the golf course. There are so many legendary stories about him that it's hard to select the best, but he also had a side to him that was completely different. He was a study in contrasts. There was the conservative side of Tommy, in which the shoes matched the sweater and the sweater matched the slacks and his clothing was of the highest quality. On the other hand he'd act like a wild man once in a while while on the golf course. He'd go berserk every now and again. He was always either throwing clubs or breaking clubs and getting fined. That is vintage Tommy.

Tommy was also a man who would not ride to the golf course in the car in the same slacks in which he was going to play. I finally got to understand the reason firsthand, much to my youthful amazement. One day we were driving to the golf course and I saw him with two pairs of slacks. I asked him why he did this and he said, "Well, son, once I put on the slacks I'm going to play in, I don't sit down in them the rest of the day because I don't want to ruin the crease."

The story of Tommy and his slacks reached the world because it happened one year while he was playing a tournament and it was really humid outside. The day hadn't been going well for Tommy at all. Suddenly he bends down and he notices that the crease has gone out of his slacks. That was it for him. He looked up at his caddie and said, "Man doesn't have to be out here playing without a crease in his slacks." Then he quit! He just walked off and withdrew because the crease had gone out of his slacks!

As a golfer, from a mechanical standpoint, Tommy is an interesting case. Tommy was truly one of the greatest swingers. If Tommy Bolt would have putted a little bit better, he might have set some unbelievable records. Even at age eighty-five he still swings the club nicely.

One of the great stories that tells volumes about Tommy's tenacity as a player happened during a practice round. On tour we have a rule that states you can't go out and hit twenty or thirty bunker shots onto a green before a tournament because it ruins the golf course for the rest of the tournament. One of the days right before the start of the tournament Tommy was out practicing, and he had been hitting two or three shots every hole out of a bunker to practice his bunker shots. Finally, one of the field staff saw this happening again and again and he came over to Tommy and told him he was going to have to fine him for hitting those extra shots. Tommy asked him how much the fine was, and the staff official told him. Suddenly Tommy dug into his pants pocket and whipped out a wad of money and tossed it near the official. The official asked in amazement what the money was for and Tommy replied, "I'm gonna keep hitting 'em!"

Tommy had a legendary reputation for throwing away clubs whenever there was a problem. In fact, even at clinics when he was teaching youngsters the fundamentals of the game of golf, he'd always teach them the right and wrong way to throw your golf club! Imagine the shocked looks on those kids' faces watching this golfing legend give them lessons on club tossing.

Tommy Bolt had a protégé in Tom Weiskopf, a great young golfer with a reputation for having a slight temper. If ESPN had had its "Shot of the Week" when both these guys were playing, they would have made "Sportscenter" every night.

As I said, I saw Tommy Bolt play when I was sixteen, and he was the first professional golfer I had ever seen in person. He took that one swing and then quit after the poor result. The second golf shot I ever saw a professional golfer take, in person, happened on the very next shot as I strolled around Tam O'Shanter that day during high school.

I was standing right beside golfer Tom Weiskopf, and I decided to watch him hit. He hit an iron shot out of the woods, and the next thing we heard was this huge roar from the crowd because the ball was one foot from the hole. I had seen his mentor Tommy Bolt's shot earlier that day and saw Tommy quit, and now I saw a professional hit a ball from the deep woods onto the green one foot from the hole. So I saw two shots. In one, a player hits a tree and quits, and in the other a player gets the ball one foot from the hole. I was in high school, and these two men had just impressed the daylights out of me. Tommy was Tom's mentor, little did I know at that point in my young life that I was witnessing the "apple not falling far from the tree."

Tom Weiskopf and I were paired together on a memorable Sunday in 1972 at the Walt Disney World Classic. I had heard all of these stories about this guy who had a temper and that his mentor and idol was Tommy Bolt. He dressed and swung the club exactly like Bolt. I was nervous playing with him because he was a terrific player with a reputation for being a little bit crazy at times.

His play was marvelous, and he looked beautiful doing it. We ended up shooting the same score that day, but what I remember most was how he took to me. He had this majestic aura about him and he told me, "Look, I really enjoyed playing with you and you're going to be a good player out here. Just keep working at it." This was the last tournament of the year, and there were a plethora of golf sponsors there to speak to players about possible upcoming endorsement opportunities the following year.

Tom Weiskopf took me by the hand and introduced me to four different golf club manufacturers and told each of them that I was going to be a good player and that they needed to speak with me and sign me. I'll never forget that day as long as I live. Here is a superstar totally going out of his way to befriend me and to help me out. It meant the world to me.

Being a tall player myself, I loved to watch him hit balls because he was one of the taller players in the game. He was six foot three and was a terrific player on tour. He had the best swing in the early 1970s. The one unforgettable aspect of Tom's game was his rhythm and balance. He could generate more power with less effort than anyone else on tour at the time. Two players could hit a five-iron that went ten feet from the hole, but his shots "looked" better than anyone else's. They were television shots. They were high and soft and had a majestic look to them.

I've always believed this swing was a combination of God-given ability and hard work. He was always in the shadow of Jack Nicklaus, being from Ohio and attending Ohio State University. I think this deeply affected him. No matter how well he played, there was always this guy named Nicklaus beating him. It's one of the things that kept him from being an even better player than he was.

In the summer of 1973 he had an incredible winning streak. He captured five PGA tour events in a two-month stretch. He won the Colonial NIT in May, the Kemper Open, the IVB-Philadelphia Golf Classic, and won the British Open and Canadian Open in July.

His father had just died and he went on a tear. I've always believed that he did this to prove to everyone what he could do in honor of his dad. Too often, the public remembers the temper flare-ups that he had on the golf course. It's sad because Tom was an incredible player with an incredible look to him. He was also, true to his idol Tommy Bolt, an impeccable dresser, and he was voted one of the best-dressed men in America. He took great pride in looking good and doing things the right way.

I don't know if Tom always got the best out of his ability, but he was a superstar. Not only was Tom a terrific player, he was a great golf course designer as well. How he approached playing the game is reflected in the designs of his golf courses. Tom always did things his way. He passed up a Ryder Cup one time because he had a chance to go on this great hunting trip and to go after a grand slam in the hunting world. Granted at this time the Ryder Cup was not the multimedia event that it is today. You can't compare the Ryder Cup back then to the Ryder Cup today with regard to importance. It has so much more significance today. I think that Tom was a guy with a lot of enthusiasm and knew what he needed to do to keep himself mentally healthy. I believe that it's healthier to do things your own way than it is to always conform to what others expect you to do and not be happy as a consequence. Tom did it "his" way. I give a guy a lot of credit for doing it his way and you've gotta love guys who do it their way. Just like Frank Sinatra.

25. Johnny Miller and Seve Ballesteros

I've played with Johnny Miller many times, and he is an interesting person. As a golfer, he is someone you'd benefit from watching on videotape, taking special note of his grip and use of irons.

Johnny Miller had a lot of confidence and a lot of ability. The secret to his success was an important combination of his grip, the speed of his club, and the squareness of his club face.

Johnny played with a fairly weak grip, but he was so aggressive and he released his body so aggressively through the hitting area, that he was able to square his club face back up again while creating a ridiculous amount of speed. He had one of the best club releases of anyone. His weaker grip allowed him to generate a lot of speed.

When I say he had a weaker grip, I don't mean that it was ridiculously so. His grip was not unlike that of other players, just slightly different than some. He played from an extremely square grip, and the result was that he did not have to manipulate the golf club to get the club face squared up. He could turn and fire like no one else, all while keeping that club face square, which is so critical for a good tee shot.

His use of irons was unparalleled. He had the ability to hit his irons the exact distance he wanted. It was an uncanny skill, and everyone took notice of it. Johnny went through a stretch of such almost perfect ball striking that he really did not have to worry about the chipping phase of golf.

He was a good putter, particularly from within ten feet. Most of his shots landed within this range for birdie and eagle putts. His shot-making during this period of time was awesome to watch. Johnny left the tour prematurely to broadcast for NBC. He had multiple problems with his legs that made it impossible for him to compete at that level.

Then there's Seve Ballesteros. Since Arnold Palmer and before Tiger Woods, there has been one player who stands out for the amount of attention devoted to him. Seve takes first prize in that category. He was aggressive beyond belief. He was strong and long. He had great imagination and was very inconsistent. He was fun to watch as a fan because of the things he'd try during a game.

On a side note, I remember when he won the 1979 British Open, at Royal Lytham and St. Annes in England, the last nine holes should have been easy. This was not the case. He drove the ball right into the middle of a parking lot! The incredible part of the story is that he made it out of the parking lot and onto the green. He just whacked that ball and sent it to where he could save par. He made the greatest shots from the worst of positions. Anything could happen with Seve on the course. Anything would happen with him out there. His recovery shots are second to none. He'd make up shots during the course of a real tournament and execute them. These shots were the kind that kids would dare each other to make out on the playground, and yet he'd try them during a major championship. He was the best at making up crazy shots. If he had played more in the United States during his career he would have been more of a cult hero with many non-golfing fans because he would have been in the paper all the time because of his antics, as he had won the World Cup at age nineteen.

Seve would chip and putt through some valley and then he'd be standing there holding the trophy at the end of the tournament. He was an exciting playmaker and one of the best in the game.

26. Gary Player

Gary Player has logged more hours on airplanes than anyone else. If he told me he had traveled five million miles, I would believe him. He has such a passion for golf.

Gary was a guy who always played the entire world. He played golf all around the globe. The fact that he won majors and was always mentioned with Nicklaus and Palmer as one of the great ones in golf is a testament to his skill. They became known as "the Big Three," all around the country and all around the world. Player's record is even more astonishing given the fact that he did this while running around the world.

"The Black Knight" is Gary's nickname. He's always worn black as a sign of strength. He was the first golfer to use weights, and when he did this weight training people thought he was nuts. They looked at him like he was loony. Look at the great shape he's in today. Many of the people who criticized him are now wishing they had his stamina and his athletic look at age sixty-five.

To leave your country and fly halfway around the world to compete is pretty impressive in my book. Gary has won major after major and yet his style has not changed. He has the same swing as he had years ago and has the same easygoing personality, which just goes to prove that winning doesn't necessarily change people.

27. Chi Chi, the Ambassador

Chi Chi Rodriguez is one of the most beloved golfers of all time, and he has been one of the greatest ambassadors the sport has ever known. When I say people enjoy his company throughout the world, this is an understatement. People love him all over the globe. He has probably performed more exhibitions and has given more clinics for children than anyone who has ever played the game of golf.

He has a great knack for teaching both older folks and little children. He's more than just a golfer. He's an entertainer. In fact, he was one of the first golfers to transcend golf and become an entertainment figure. He's made an awful lot of people happy and his golf game has been terrific.

He treats the corporations to some special clinics, and in his clinic he entertains them. He hits trick shots, does imitations, and gives lessons. You get to learn golf and have a good time.

There was one time where he hit one ball with a big high slice and then immediately hit another ball that hooked inward and the two collided in midair! I personally saw him do it! Can you believe that? Chi Chi is the ultimate performer.

Chi Chi, in my book, is also Mr. Charity. His foundation helps tons of underprivileged children, and he is one of the main reasons why the SENIOR PGA TOUR was so successful. He won tournaments and entertained the fans over the years, but has not forgotten where the future of golf lies—with our children.

28. The Golden Bear

I started my golf personality memories off with Arnold and I'm finishing this section of the book with Jack.

Jack Nicklaus hit a lot of one-irons and three-woods and would often lay up off the tee. I once asked him why he did this and how he decided that this was the correct strategy for him. He told me that the process was simple. He would stand on the tee and look at a hole and decide if the driver was a shot he was really comfortable with, and if it wasn't because of either bunkers or creeks or hazards, then he would ask himself whether a three-wood or a one-iron would work better for him. He'd work his way back from club to club until he selected the one that was right for him from a distance standpoint and from a control standpoint. Jack rarely misses fairways. He was the best player we've ever seen in the history of golf and he only used his driver for 50 percent of the driving holes. Most amateurs think the driver is the only club to tee it up with on par 4's and 5's. Jack understood the importance of placing the ball on the fairway, and this was his secret to becoming the greatest golfer in the twentieth century. Jack gave away fewer shots than anybody else and he was the best in course management.

Do you ever remember him hitting the ball into the water or having to play miracle shots because he was too aggressive? The answer is a resounding no. Many times he was criticized for being a bit boring because he was so consistent. He would drive the ball onto the fairway and then hit the ball onto the green, and end up making a fantastic birdie putt. To me, this kind of golf was exciting because Jack showed us all how to be better strategists. He was the king of golf strategy. He was the first player on tour to use a yardage book. Here was a man who would actually go out and pace off the course by foot. He knew the yardage from point to point on each hole.

Jack not only raised a great family, but he has always had a varied amount of interests aside from golf. He always spent a lot of time with his family. The family went on safaris in Africa, and they went skiing. They did a lot of neat things.

Jack Nicklaus will go down in history as one of the greatest golfers of all time, and yet he still took time away from the game to be with his family.

When I first came on tour in 1972, Jack and I were talking about the entire concept behind practicing. I noticed that everyone had a different approach to the practice rounds and to practicing after a round. I was sort of confused as to what I was supposed to do, given that there were countless theories on what the practice rounds were designed to do and how they should be handled.

Jack told me that to just go out and hit balls for four or five hours wasn't always the answer. That was not what the practice rounds were all about in his opinion. He reassured me that quality practice was what was most important. He told me how I needed to understand what worked for me and to stay within that system. The great players know themselves, according to him. For him, he told me, he'd hit ten or fifteen balls to warm up, but once he was warmed up if he'd hit eight or ten shots exactly like he wanted to, he'd quit.

"What good does it do to just stand out here and keep hitting balls?" he asked me rhetorically. "If I could do what I want to do and it works for about ten shots, why do anything differently?" he explained to me. If he wasn't hitting well, he felt the same way about the practice rounds. He might sit down and regroup and think about some mental changes.

This talk came at a point in my career during which I would go and hit balls for two or three hours at a time, and a lot of times I'd hit two full buckets of balls after a round just because I was angry. It wouldn't do me any good, other than to let off steam and get rid of frustration. He told me if I wanted to pound some golf balls and let off steam, that was fine. Just don't confuse this with good practice. If I really wanted to focus, then keep the practices short. Jack was a great believer in short, focused practice sessions rather than long, unfocused ones.

After the Grand Slam in 1979 in Rochester, New York, I was lucky enough to catch a ride home on Jack's airplane. This was memorable because I finally had him all to myself for a length of time where I could actually speak to him about golf. We once again spoke about practicing and he, again, stressed his theory on practice. Practice was merely a warm-up to him, and if things went well, he would quit because anything else is futile. This was the second time this was said to me by him. I now was convinced that he was correct. He also had a theory that it's perfectly acceptable to leave the golf course and come back with a clear head. Don't just stand there at the practice range in vapor lock. Leave, go back to the office, and then come back. Leave, go home, and then come back when you're ready.

If I had to distill all of my private conversations with him into one overarching theme, I would say that the most important thing to Jack Nicklaus is focus. He was one of the best minds in golf and never gave less than his best effort. Michael Jordan is like Jack Nicklaus because he also never gives anything less than 100 percent. If the best player in the world does this, it sends a signal to the rest of us.

Part Four

Parting Putts

Golf has given me a life I couldn't possibly have imagined at age twelve. I thought I'd close this book with some parting thoughts on this great game called golf.

29. The Armchair Golfer

The armchair golfer should become acquainted with *golf etiquette* and the wonderful theory behind these words.

Golf etiquette is a combination of demeanor and knowing the rules of golf. A proper demeanor should start from within yourself. You shouldn't be rude to others in life, so don't be rude to them on the golf course. Be considerate.

There are a few important rules of golf that everyone, from the corporate golfer to the occasional weekend golfer, needs to know before you begin to play. Rather than inundating you with all of the rules of golf, let me take you through an entire hole from start to finish from an etiquette standpoint.

The first crazy thing most amateurs do is they make sure all their clubs are legal, and yet they don't abide by any rules once on the course. Almost no amateur plays by the rules. They take illegal drops, whack the ball on the fairway to get a better lie, and don't putt out their putts. To me the rules are important, but having fun is also important. Don't confuse having fun on the golf course, however, with playing the game called golf. If you're having a lot of fun not marking your ball and not putting out four-foot putts, then that's terrific. It's not golf, however. Golf is a game where ALL putts are to be putted. It doesn't matter who's behind you. You should putt out every single putt. There are no gimmes on the PGA TOUR.

Amateur weekend golfers forget to mark their ball and they take mulligans like mad. Many times they won't display proper golf etiquette, forgetting to rake sand traps after they've blasted out of the sand and forgetting to repair ball marks. They also won't yell "fore" if their balls go off on some other fairway. They'll take illegal water drops, and they'll not count strokes. There's nothing wrong with being slaphappy and having a blast at the golf course, but it's not golf. Golf is golf. Not counting strokes is outside the game, but if that's what floats your boat, that's fine as well.

First, you approach your tee shot. You must tee-off in between the markers and behind them. There is a two-club-length area that must be observed. You should stand still and be quiet while others in your group are teeing-off. Don't move around or rattle the change in your pocket. Don't take practice swings so the players around you hear the swooshing of the club. Keep out of vision of the player teeing-off, and when he or she is done with their tee shot, approach the tee and tee-off yourself. If you're using a cart, don't park the cart in front of the tee-off area.

After you've found your ball, hopefully in the fairway, the golfer farthest back hits first, and so on. This not only makes sense, but it makes for safer golf play. When you hit your iron or your wood, replace your divot. If it's a good-sized divot, put it back unless it's Bermuda grass. Bermuda grass doesn't grow back. In that case you should use the sand-fillers that come on the backs of the golf carts and replace the divot with sand so that the grass can grow again in that area. (Bermuda grass grows inwards from the edges, and so replacing the divot with sand allows the grass to regrow.) Don't wander around while others are taking their iron shots or wood shots. Show respect to them.

Water hazards and drop areas come into play often during a round. A golfer needs to know the rules for the lateral water hazards and the regular water hazards. There is a difference as the rules allow you in the case of a regular water hazard to treat it as a yellow hazard and play the ball, keeping the hazard between you and the hole. On a lateral hazard, or a red hazard, you are able to sometimes go to the side of the hazard depending on where the ball crossed as it went into the water. You won't always have to re-hit over water.

I strongly recommend joining the USGA, and receiving a copy of the USGA rules of golf. The rules are not there to penalize you. The rules are there to help you, and more often than not they do, because by knowing the rules you will know when you might be afforded relief when you most need it. This is especially true when it comes to out of bounds, trees, and water hazards, or even fences.

Once on the green you need to address some basic rules. First, when you walk up onto the green the first thing you should do is fix the ball mark. This is an important part of golf etiquette both for you and for the groups behind you. The ball mark is the mark the ball makes on the green as it initially hits the green. Some of the players

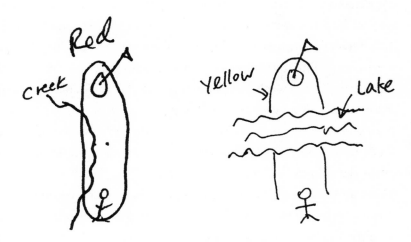

punch the mark up and then tap it down with the head of their putter (the flat part). Others just tap it down. Either way you want the green to be smooth for the next group of players.

Second, you need to know how to mark your ball. When the ball stops rolling you need to mark it with a coin. The mark must be placed on the spot where the ball ended up after it finished its roll, directly behind the ball. Whoever is farthest from the hole on the green putts first. You need to wait for everyone to be on the green, as in the case where someone is chipping onto the green, before you begin putting. Once you are ready to putt, you are allowed to take your time, but you should not take an excessive amount of time. I would recommend taking the proper time necessary to figure the break in the green and the speed of the green and putt accordingly and play out. Don't overdramatize the situation and spend an hour trying to figure out the break. Too much time spent on analyzing a putt just confuses you.

I've often been asked about how to properly care for your golf clubs. I like to wipe off the grips and heads with a wet towel. It's also a good idea to use a wooden tee to clean the grooves on the irons and woods. By running the wooden tee's pointed end through the grooves and extracting the mud and dirt from the grooves your club faces will have a better bite to them when they strike the ball. You can scrub the clubs down once a week, but I clean my clubs while I'm playing. I wipe the heads off after every shot. This way the dirt that gets on the heads does not accumulate and become embedded into the club heads. By leaving the dirt in the club heads for a weekly cleanup you run the risk of the dirt adhering to the club's surface.

It's proper etiquette to clean your club heads while you're walking, if you're carrying your clubs over your shoulder. If you're not walking with the bag on your back, and you're not using a pull cart, then clean them when you approach the next hole, just not while you're driving the golf cart. These simple rules will allow you to enjoy the game of golf and to enjoy the company of those with whom you're playing.

You're finished with your round, and now it's time to sit down in front of the TV and watch the pros play.

To sit home and watch golf on television you need a great remote control and an ample supply of food at your seat. You can't watch golf and run off and get something to eat every two minutes. Only kidding. But seriously, you need to really watch the pros swing and see how they keep their left arms straight and how the trunk of their body generates the necessary speed to achieve maximum distance.

If you're intent on trying to improve your game you need to watch the rhythm and balance of the players. Very seldom do the men and women at the professional level overswing. You need to also notice golf course management and how a player attacks each hole: aggressive versus conservative. Try to analyze when a player is aggressive and why he chose to be aggressive. Try to also notice when that player is being conservative and why that might be the case as well.

When it comes to putting, watching the players putt is crucial. You can learn a lot by watching the PGA and LPGA players line up putts and figure breaks and speeds of the green. You can also learn to perfect that pendulum motion that is so crucial to putting. When watching putting, watch the speed of the putts. Very seldom does a professional player have to make a five- or six-footer for a two-putt. They know how to touch the ball with that club face such that the ball drops into the cup. The ball is always dying around the hole with great speed, leaving the professional with non-stressful par putts. You're not going to get stressed out tapping in a one-foot putt.

When a player is really playing well, notice how easy it looks on television. If the player does get in trouble, see how they recover from trouble. They don't just take a five-wood when they're in the trees hoping that it gets through. They are playing some sort of shot out of trouble. They are playing a specific shot out of trouble, so notice how many of those times when a golfer starts out in trouble he or she still ends up parring or making birdie on the hole.

The amateur should watch the pros on television and learn that a bad shot is not the end of the world. They can use their creativity to get out of trouble. Creativity is an important aspect to winning in golf. Sometimes players choke up on the club and sometimes they don't alter anything.

The demeanor of the players is another important facet of the game of golf that should be taken notice of by amateurs. The average golfer is screaming and yelling at the local club or state course, while the pro is taking things in stride for the most part, with some rare exceptions.

Bruce Devlin, a great friend of mine, was playing in a tournament in San Diego one year and he was doing very well until he came to the eighteenth hole. It's a par-5 hole that can, under normal circumstances, be reached with two shots. Well, he knocked the ball into the water. It was demoralizing and he had to take the water hazard drop behind the water and ended up knocking it into the water yet again. He had to take another drop behind the water and, you guessed it, hit the ball into the water one more time. Before he knew it, he had eleven strokes for the hole. These guys are good, but the craziest things still happen to the best of us.

In 2001 a bizarre event happened at the British Open involving Ian Woosnam, a very good golfer. He was rolling along and was in contention for a possible win on Sunday when he was penalized two strokes, a considerable amount in a major, for having more than the fourteen clubs that every golfer on tour is allowed in their golf bag. There have been players who have been penalized for having a child's club in their bag because their kid was practicing on the practice green the day before and they forgot to take out their kid's club. Even though everyone can see that this club is designed for a child, it's still considered a club in the golfer's bag, and if it places the golfer's fourteen club limit in jeopardy, then the golfer will be penalized. This was a major, however, and the club was a driver, so it was pretty conspicuous and the officials on the sidelines spotted it and the head official came over and assessed the penalty, much to the dismay of Woosnam. When you watch golf on television you must notice all of the goings-on. The amateur might be playing a country club with a business friend and that friend might check their bag and say that they have too many clubs in their bag and want them to deduct some strokes. If it can happen to Woosnam in the British Open, it could happen to any weekend golfer.

Sometimes I think fans enjoy watching us mess up, and they love to watch the U.S. Open because anything can happen. The conditions of the U.S. Open are so difficult that when players end up being in the rough, they never recover. More than any other fan, the golf fan is intrigued by the fact that we are all beatable on any given hole. The armchair golfer knows that if he hits his best shot, he can beat us on any given hole. It's possible for the amateur to beat Jack Nicklaus on a given hole. It won't happen more than once in one hundred times, but there is the possibility.

30. The Changing Game of Golf

Golf has changed considerably over the last thirty years. Back when I was playing golf at the beginning of my career, the game was more one of finesse. Part of the reason was the golf course conditions. The courses were firmer and faster and the quality of grass on the golf courses was inferior to that of today. This made for playing creative shots because the balls had a more free bounce to them. The game, from a conditions standpoint, has changed so much that it makes for easier watching on television. Good shots end up where they should end up, but it was not so thirty years ago. Thus, the power game, or the play-in-the-air strategy, is more prevalent today. This makes for more exciting golf for the fans, however. Fans watching the game on television are seeing some great drives. Equipment has made for longer games and for more interesting fan participation.

The graphite shafts, the longer-sized clubs, and the heads of the clubs have all changed, thus affecting our game. Titanium came along and made for a beautiful marriage with the game of golf. However, the one area that has changed more than any one single area in golf has been the golf ball.

The golf ball has changed drastically over the years. Balls today don't curve nearly as much as they did years ago. The balls are more stable and are easier to play in the wind. The manufacturers have created a new design of golf ball. The core is a solid core, and the golf ball covers are different in many cases so as to change the spin rate. We knew nothing about spin rates and launch angles years ago.

These new testing centers that diagnose your golf game are incredible. They can figure out the best ball for you to play and the best shafts to use. They basically have you swing with your natural stroke and you are plugged up to these computerized machines, which in turn analyze your swing and stroke.

I've had diagnostics done on myself. The machine tells you how you're swinging the club. In certain cases you might be spinning the ball too much, as the computer knows what the optimum spin rate is in general. The outcome could be that you could have a specially made driver that would allow you to use your natural stroke and, because of the makeup of the driver, the club will compensate for your overspinning the ball. A golf club manufacturer can do this just about any problem you could have. It's a toy store for golf. The pros get the clubs made to their specifications. Obviously if you're a CEO and money is no object, you can have clubs made to your specification. But what about the majority of golfers for whom money *is* an object? The diagnostic exams can still better your game because they'll find out what your strengths and weaknesses are, and then you can buy clubs accordingly.

The marketing of the game has changed, and it started changing with Ely Calloway and Greg Norman. Greg Norman was the first golfer to mass market his products and logo and namesake. Business and golf now go together quite well. He marketed himself and created opportunities in an era after Arnold Palmer, and the public gravitated to him. The result was that he was able to capitalize on his popularity and success and make a ton of money. Today you can go into stores and see shark clothing everywhere either bearing his name or logo of the shark, or even both. I say this because Greg helped market golf and bring golf to the department stores through his creativity and his popularity. Ely Calloway, likewise, helped bring the game of golf to a new generation of young golfers. Other companies soon followed by targeting their products to a diverse group of young golfers, and kids became more interested in golf equipment and going to the driving ranges. The only way for the game of golf to grow is to market it to children all over the country. Children in inner cities and all over the nation as well as those in the suburbs must be made to feel that they are the future of golf.

31. The LPGA Goes Television

Judy Rankin and JoAnne Carner started bringing the LPGA to television and helped change the face of women's golf forever. Women's golf has received more and more national attention each year. Karrie Webb became the youngest woman to win a Grand Slam and she will go down in history as one of the greatest.

In my early years on the tour, Judy Rankin was queen on the LPGA Tour. She was so accurate with her driving ability that I've often said she could drive that golf ball through a key hole. She hit many great shots and was a great chipper and putter. She really made the best of her ability.

JoAnne Carner was the first long hitter on the LPGA. She had these incredible long drives in the early 1970s. She overpowered everyone with her strength and length. Judy was a bit more of a finesse player. It became fun to follow her drives, and it made for exciting golf that seemed right for television.

These two ladies used their diverse styles of golf to clean up on the LPGA throughout the 1970s. The ladies controlled ladies' golf for ten to fifteen years. Both women not only cared about the game but also had great personalities and class. They changed the way fans viewed women's golf. Judy has become a terrific broadcaster and both were inducted into the Hall of Fame. Judy's a good friend of mine, and she has done so much for the game of golf. These two women have also done much to get the corporate sponsorship that placed the LPGA in the lucrative position in which it now rests.

JoAnne and Judy set the table and then came Nancy Lopez, one of the all-time greatest. Nancy was, and still is, Ms. Personality.

Nancy Lopez hit the scene with a golf swing that was different, and it captivated everyone. She had the nice smile and the enthusiasm to match it. She raised the bar for many years from the late 1970s into the early 1990s in women's golf. Her run is reminiscent of Jack Nicklaus's run on the PGA. To this day Nancy still takes the young kids to school on the golf course. She will continue to win, and it's all because of her conditioning and her approach to the game. She has been instrumental in getting the major corporate sponsors to bring the LPGA further into the cable and direct television markets. Nancy always takes the time to sign autographs, and she genuinely loves her fans.

Patti Berg, though from a different era, really helped sell women's golf as well to the younger generation. She had a tremendous clinic, which I attended. She was an interesting woman with a phenomenal swing. She actually helped promote the game in a more vigorous manner than anyone else through marketing and sponsorship. She was one of the first women to forcefully make corporations aware of the tremendous marketing power of the LPGA.

Mickey Wright and Kathy Whitworth were the two dominant stars in the era right before television discovered the LPGA. No one has dominated the LPGA at one time like those two ladies.

Annika Sorenstam is the current standard for young women today. She was the first Swedish player to win the U.S. Women's Open in 1995. She's so straight and almost never misses a fairway and never misses a green. I think people can learn a lot from watching her because she doesn't overpower golf courses, but she places the ball exceptionally well. She's not a flamboyant or dramatic player, but she is a consistent tee-to-green player.

ESPN and the major networks are now televising more LPGA golf than ever before. It's great to see, because for a while these women competed and only received praise in the newspapers. Now they are able to enjoy the national and worldwide acclaim they deserve, but regrettably still not to the degree that they deserve.

However, something happened in 2001 that merits attention for two reasons. First, it's one of the most monumental events in golf, and, second, it's been overlooked. Karrie Webb became the youngest to win all four majors on the LPGA. This was such a great accomplishment, and my heartfelt congratulations go out to her. Why, however, did she receive only about two minutes of national press coverage? David Duval won the British Open and the papers were talking about it for days. I'm not taking anything away from the guys, but what Webb did was unbelievable. She is one of the top young athletes in any sport, and it is troublesome that this was not given more press coverage. People have asked me why this has happened and I have no answer. I am troubled by the media's not giving her more credit. Is it the sponsors? Is it the nature of television? Selectivity of content? Does the public want to hear this story, or do the sponsors control what the public hears? Do advertising dollars speak too loudly or not loud enough?

I believe that many men and women do want to hear about Karrie Webb's accomplishment. Cover stories could have been done about her, and marketing could have been done to further highlight her feat to the world. Right now, Karrie and Annika are the young phenoms of the LPGA, and more young stars are being born to continue carrying the torch.

32. My Favorites

MY FAVORITE SHORT PAR 3'S

- Hole 7, Pebble Beach
- Hole 12, Augusta (The Masters)
- Hole 15, Cypress Point
- Hole 17, TPC Sawgrass
- Hole 11, St. Andrews

The seventh hole at Pebble Beach is only 100 yards long. It plays downhill. So how hard can it be? Unfortunately it has a small green surrounded by bunkers with the ocean left, long, and to the right. The big issue on this hole is always the wind. There are days when you can hit a sand wedge to this hole, and there are days when I've hit four-irons. Combine the problems with the wind, the smallness of this green, and the rugged beauty of the ocean, and it's a terrific hole.

The twelfth hole at Augusta plays right at 150 yards. It may be the hardest eight-iron shot you'll ever have to play, because of the swirling winds. There is a creek that runs right in front of the green, and there's a bunker behind it. The winds blow down either the eleventh or thirteenth fairway, into the trees, and then swirl around. Judging the club you want to hit there on certain days is almost impossible. Again, the two *w*'s, water and wind, make the hole exciting.

The fifteenth hole at Cypress Point is one which oftentimes people don't pay much attention to because of the sixteenth hole there, the long par 3, which we'll talk about later. The green and tee here hang over the edge of the ocean. The waves come crashing up onto the rocks. The green is two levels with bunkers surrounding it, and it's tucked right into the rocks of the ocean and the shrubs of the hillside. It's a beautiful hole that can be treacherous at the same time.

The seventeenth at TPC Sawgrass has a green totally surrounded by water. Even though you're hitting a wedge or a nine-iron, it's still a scary shot because of all the water. If you put it in the water, just re-tee it. This hole, on a calm day, is pretty straightforward. When the fronts come in, the wind blows from left to right, making you hit seven-irons and six-irons to this hole. When that happens, balls galore end up in the water.

The eleventh hole at St. Andrews is an elevated green with a huge, deep pot bunker that guards the front of the green. If you put the ball in this bunker, you have absolutely no chance to get the ball up and in. The water behind this green and the wind both play havoc with this hole.

MY FAVORITE LONG PAR 3'S
- Hole 17, Pebble Beach (from the U.S. Open tee)
- Hole 5, Whitemarsh
- Hole 16, Cypress Point
- Hole 17, Bay Hill Country Club
- Hole 16, Westchester Country Club

The seventeenth hole at Pebble Beach from the tee they use at the U.S. Open is basically two small greens hooked together with a ridge. Bunkers surround the green. Ocean is left and back of this green. Probably the most famous long iron ever hit was hit by Jack Nicklaus in the 1972 U.S. Open when he hit a one-iron and it hit the pin and stopped a foot from the hole, and he went on to win the U.S. Open.

The fifth hole at Whitemarsh is probably even too long of a hole: There's a creek on the right, and bunkers guard the cup. It plays in the 240–250-yard range. This hole was so difficult that when we used to play the IVB Whitemarsh back in the 1970s, players hit one- and two-irons. If they absolutely drilled them, they could run up to the front of the green. If they stayed just short of the green, they'd pitch on and take their chances of making a three or four. If they tried to hit with a driver, they made a lot of fives on this hole.

The sixteenth hole at Cypress Point is maybe the most famous long par 3 ever. It's a hole where on a calm day you have to hit a 230-yard shot over part of the ocean. The green is stuck out on the rocks along the beach. There are days when, if they have to hit into the wind, the best players in the world can't hit it over the water, and they have to lay up. On those days you lay to the left with a four- or five-iron and then play a wedge. It's hard to believe that the best players who have ever played this game don't even shoot at the green on a par 3. This is the case half the time you play this hole. Even if you hit two balls in the water, you still think it's a rugged and beautiful hole.

The seventeenth at Bay Hill Country Club plays over 200 yards from an elevated tee. There is a small pond to the right of the green, and bunkers guard the hole. It's a par 3 that requires you to play just an absolute perfect shot to put it on the green. I was playing with Don

Pooly in the Bay Hill Classic there and he made a hole-in-one and won a million dollars.

The sixteenth hole at Westchester Country Club is another par 3 in the 200-yard range played from an elevated tee. The green slopes from back to front. It's a fairly basic-looking hole, but it's so difficult because there are two bunkers that guard each side of the green. If you miss the green to the right or left, you have a very difficult time making par. The best way to play this hole is to keep the ball on the very front of the green; if you miss the green, miss it short. From there it's a pretty easy up and in. I birdied this hole when I won here in 1977. The smart player will play a two-iron shot off the tee. This puts you in perfect position for a par.

MY FAVORITE SHORT PAR 4'S

- Hole 10, Riviera Country Club
- Hole 17, TPC Scottsdale
- Hole 9, Harbour Town (Hilton Head Island)
- Hole 10, Westchester Country Club
- Hole 1, Cherry Hills

The tenth hole at the Riviera Country Club is a par 4 that's not much over 300 yards. Under the right conditions, you could probably try to drive this green, but that's not necessarily the smartest play. Even after you've hit a long iron down the fairway, it's very important to put the ball in the very left-hand edge of the fairway so that you have a nice angle for your second shot. Even if it's a wedge or sand wedge, the green is only about twenty-five feet wide with bunkers on both sides. It's one of the most challenging seventy- or eighty-yard wedge shots you'll have to play.

The seventeenth hole at TPC Scottsdale is one of the newer holes on this list. Bunkers guard the fairway, and there's a pot bunker right in the middle of the fairway that you have to avoid. You either lay up short of this bunker, or you try to drive it over the bunker, and if you try to drive it over there's a good chance that you get onto the green. There's a pond that guards the left part of the green. It's a hole where you can drive it on and give yourself a decent putt to make two or three, but if you hit a poor shot and put it in the pot bunker or the lake you'll make five or six. Andrew Magee in the 2000 Phoenix Open was attempting to drive this green. The group in front of him was still putting. He drove it up onto the green, it ricocheted off of one of the players in front of his putter and went into the hole for a hole in one.

The ninth hole at Harbour Town (Hilton Head Island) is another 300-yardish hole. There is no chance to drive on this one. Pine trees guard front left of the green and also the right side of the fairway. It's a horseshoe-shaped green with a very small target. You have to play a perfect iron off the tee, probably a four-iron, to give yourself a wedge shot for a second shot. It's one of those holes that you have to be so precise on because of the horseshoe shape of the green and the bunker in the middle of the green. It's only about twenty feet wide in the areas that you need to hit your shot.

The tenth at Westchester Country Club is a hole you'll see players drive on once in a while. It has a very small green. Bunkers guard both sides. Trees are on the right, two or three huge trees on the left. The green sits on a ridge and slopes dramatically off on the left, so any drive to the left makes you not only mess with the hill and the trees, but with deep rough. It's a hole that if you were to play the percentages, you'd play a one- or two-iron or a fairway wood down the fairway about fifty yards short of the green, and then just play a sand wedge on from there.

The first hole at Cherry Hills was made legendary by Arnold Palmer when he drove the green in the 1960 U.S. Open. He went on to shoot

65 in the final round to win. The creek guards the right hand side of the fairway. It has a small green. The hole looks tame, but it's one of those holes you remember more for the history of it than the hole itself.

MY FAVORITE LONG PAR 4'S
- Hole 18, Oakland Hills (U.S. Open tee)
- Hole 8, Pebble Beach
- Hole 17, St. Andrews
- Hole 5, Colonial
- Hole 18, Harbour Town (Hilton Head Island)

The eighteenth hole at Oakland Hills has a dogleg to the right. It's a very long par 5 converted into a par 4 for the U.S. Opens. Bunkers guard both sides of the fairway. It's a difficult drive, and even after a great drive you're still left with a second shot in the 170- to 200-yard range to a green that's very undulating and slopes dramatically from back to front. It's a tough second shot—and once you get to the green it's even tougher putting.

The eighth hole at Pebble Beach is probably the most famous hole in golf. It's a par 4 that plays roughly 440 yards. Your tee shot is a semi-blind tee shot that you play with a driver or a three-wood up to the top of a bluff. Then you shoot over the corner of the ocean to a very, very small green, which is guarded by bunkers on all sides. You're playing a second shot in the 170- to 200-yard range. It's a very, very difficult second shot not only because of the shot itself, but because of the distractions of the ocean.

The seventeenth hole at St. Andrews is called the Road Hole. It's very unusual, in that you actually drive over the corner of the Old Course Hotel. Even after missing the hotel and hitting it in the fairway, you're left with a long second shot in the 170- to 190-yard range to a green that has a road right on the back edge of the green and a very, very deep pot bunker that guards the front of the green. Almost any shot that lands over that pot bunker is going to run through the green onto the road. Many, many British Opens have been lost on this hole.

The fifth hole at Colonial is a long par 4 dogleg to the right. The river runs along the right-hand side. It's a very narrow driving hole with trees on the left. A lot of players will hit drivers on this hole, and others will play three-woods or one-irons. If you take the more conservative root, with a one-iron or three-wood off the tee, you going to be left with a shot in the 220-yard range. The green is surrounded by bunkers, big trees, and water on the right.

The eighteenth hole at Harbour Town (Hilton Head Island) is one of the most picturesque finishing holes. You drive over a marsh into a wide driving area. The marsh continues along the left-hand side of the hole, and the green is surrounded by marsh on the left and bunkers on the right. The famous Harbor Town lighthouse is in the background and it's picturesque, but when you're playing into the wind, it's very difficult to hit the ball onto the green.

MY FAVORITE PAR 5'S
- Hole 18, Pebble Beach
- Hole 16, Firestone
- Hole 13 and Hole 15, Augusta (The Masters)
- Hole 14, St. Andrews
- Hole 11, TPC Sawgrass

The eighteenth hole at Pebble Beach is famous because the Pacific Ocean runs the entire length of the hole on the left. For years and years there were huge pine trees that guarded the right of this green. They have unfortunately died, which has made the hole play a little bit easier and given players a chance to reach the green in two. The sheer beauty of the hole, and the fact that it's the last hole of the course, make the experience rewarding. The beauty of the scene itself, the history of the hole, and the fact that it's the last hole are all distractions making for a nice golfing experience.

The sixteenth hole at Firestone was dubbed the Monster years ago when no one could get there in two. The hole is 625 yards long and has a small pond that guards the front of the green. Most players have to hit two great shots to put themselves in position for a wedge shot as their third shot. Only a handful of players can ever hit it on the green in regulation. Nicklaus and Woods have both done it.

I've put the thirteenth and fifteenth holes at Augusta in as a combination for good reason, because the Masters is probably decided 99 percent of the time by these two holes on Sunday. Both holes have water on them, and both are reachable in two. We've seen, over the history of the holes, lots of eagles, and lots of sixes and sevens. Not very often do you play two par 5's in a three-hole stretch that you can either make an eagle or a double bogey on.

The fourteenth at St. Andrews is a par 5 with a stone wall on the right that's out of bounds. Hell's bunker is on this hole. There are bunkers everywhere. It's one of the holes where you can play it downwind and it doesn't seem like it's that difficult a hole because it's easy to carry your second shot over Hell's bunker. If the wind turns into you, and you've never played it under those conditions, you'll have no idea how to play the hole. The green is difficult to putt and is also surrounded by bunkers. The more the wind blows, the more challenging the hole becomes.

The eleventh hole at TPC Sawgrass may not be one of the greatest holes in terms of beauty and history, but it's an interesting par 5 in that after you hit your tee shot down the fairway, you have two options on how to play the hole. There are a lake and a deep bunker that guard the right side of the green. Where the hole is placed on the green determines how you play your second shot. You can go to the right, you can go to the left, or you can try to hit this green in two. You have three options, and that's what I think is so neat about this hole. It gives the player a lot of options. It's a hole where with two great shots you can make an eagle, and with a poor shot you can make a six or seven very easily.

MY FAVORITE GOLF COURSES
- Cypress Point
- Muirfield Village
- Winged Foot
- Medina Number 3
- Harbour Town (Hilton Head Island)
- Pebble Beach (on a nice day)
- Cherry Hills
- St. Andrews
- Muirfield (Scotland)
- Westchester Country Club

If there's a course I could play every day of my life, I'd pick Cypress Point. It has a great variety of golf holes. It's always in nice condition, and it has the sheer beauty of three or four holes playing along the ocean. I guess it might be Golfing Heaven on earth.

Muirfield Village is one of the best courses Nicklaus has ever done. It's a golf course where every single hole is interesting. You can see everything in front of you. There aren't a lot of tricks. It has great natural beauty, with creeks and ponds throughout, not to mention big oak trees. It also has one of the great practice ranges. The range is one giant circle and you can hit under any wind condition. The practice range also has practice bunkers and practice greens. It's perfect. Most importantly, they have the best milkshakes and brownies in the locker room of any place in the country.

Winged Foot is a typical U.S. Open–type golf course that they have played a lot of major championships on, and it's cut through a lot of big oak trees. There aren't a lot of tricks. The tenth hole here has an elevated green with deep bunkers surrounding the hole. Ben Hogan always spoke of this hole as one of his favorite par 3 holes. The course is a friendly place. Winged Foot says to you on the first tee, "Hey, come and play me and see what you can do!"

Medina Number 3 is a course much like Winged Foot. It has huge oak trees and great facilities. There are three courses there, and my favorite is the Number 3. It is a natural course in all respects. However, if you are not driving the ball well there, you might as well get a cab and go home. You have no chance of playing well on this course if you're not in the fairway. The course has been carved out of what seems to be a whole forest. Even the par 5 holes are tough. One par 5 hole here is 600 yards long. The par 3 holes are very difficult, and three of the four holes play over a river that runs through the body of the course. The second, seventeenth, and eighteenth holes all play hard. You have to hit terrific shots, and there isn't much leeway. Every one of those greens slopes back to front, and there's water on the short side as well. You can't be short. It's a Catch-22: You need to be perfect here or you're done. However, the big oak trees make for the feel of a private golfing experience. You'll feel as if you have the course to yourself, since you don't see the groups in front of you because of the layout.

Harbour Town on Hilton Head Island is a wonderful combination of short holes and long holes. There are short par 3's and long par 3's. This course has the best set of four par 3's that I've ever played.

．　．　．

Pebble Beach is probably the most beautiful golf course around on a nice day. Most courses I like have a combination of short holes and long holes, hard holes and easy holes. Pebble Beach is exactly this way. There are so many nice facets to the course. The hardest part about playing Pebble Beach is keeping your concentration and not watching the seals and the Pacific Ocean and the boats out in the water. The ninth hole is difficult in and of itself and with mental fatigue if you've just played the eighth hole and had a bad day there. Often the eighth hole will be so fatiguing that many pros lose their concentration on the ninth hole. To conquer the ninth, examine and take into account the wind. There is no substitute for good driving on this hole. Lay up short of the green and treat the hole as a par 5. Aside from that advice on that particular hole, rather than worry about your score on each hole, just enjoy the ambience of the course. You'll be missing out on a lot of beautiful scenery and good times with your friends if you don't stop to look around.

Cherry Hills is such a historic course. Arnold Palmer won his U.S. Open there in grand fashion. It's a course close to my heart, because I won my first U.S. Open there in 1978. What sets this course apart from all others is that when you first play it, you think it's not that difficult. However, the more you play the course the more you appreciate its subtleties. It has some short holes early on, and it gets harder and harder as the round progresses. What makes this course special is that from the clubhouse and the first and tenth tees the whole backdrop is the Rocky Mountains. The view of those snowcapped peaks while you're teeing off is something to behold.

St. Andrews is the home of golf. It is the oldest course in the world. To think that people thought about golf and built this course hundreds of years ago! To play that same course makes you feel as if you are part of history. The history of the course and its beautiful surroundings make playing it exciting. The winds change every single day, and there are hundreds of bunkers. You could play a round of golf here one day and, because of the wind factor, you could go back the next day and see bunkers you never knew existed.

Muirfield in Scotland is another British Open golf course, and it, too, has a lot of history. It's the home of the 2002 British Open. This course has a lot of blind shots that you'll like because you're in Scotland and it's fun. The wind has a huge effect on how you play the golf course. There's also a lot of deep rough.

Westchester is very close to my heart, too, because I had my first win there on tour in 1977. The course plays much like U.S. Open golf courses. It has a lot of deep rough and different types of holes. It has a good combination of short par 3's, long par 3's, short par 4's, and long par 4's. It's a wonderful golfing experience, with greens that are difficult to putt, but also a golf course where you have to drive your ball very well. The Buick Classic is held here, and it draws many fans for its friendliness and its intimacy. The course has the eleventh hole with the creek that comes into play; it's a nice par 4. Make sure you steer clear of the creek and then you'll have a nice 180-yard uphill shot to a green guarded by bunkers. Don't let the scenery go by the wayside here. The beauty of the course should be as enjoyable as the idea of playing well.

33. Designing Your Dream

Even in ninth grade I used to doodle drawings of golf holes in the backs of my books. I felt about my doodlings the same way an artist feels about his sketches.

Designing a golf course and observing its every step during development is a terrific feeling. The jubilation felt when the course opens to the public or to the members of the club is tremendous. As the designer, I feel as if I'm the father of a newborn child. It's a terrific and rewarding feeling that I have cherished over the years. I'm still very much involved in golf course design, and I've designed many courses over the years. Golf course design is not easy, and there are many steps in the process.

There are also some anxious moments along the way because you can't go back once the bulldozers start digging up earth. When I started designing golf courses with Roger Packard, sometimes the modifications I wanted made could not be physically done because of irrigation problems. The underground aspect of designing is quite intricate. Then there was the question of dollars and cents—the bottom line. Understanding budgets is another important ingredient in building a golf course. I might want to make the dogleg a certain way because the land lends itself visually to naturally bending that way. Underground irrigation might be another story.

The purpose of becoming involved in golf course design, for me, was to be able to build a course that is fun and playable for every level of player. Adding a shorter tee isn't always the answer. Positioning of bunkers where you force the amateur to make these incredible carry shots is another story. There are also questions of forced carry shots over lakes, canyons, and rivers. These are important factors to consider with regard to golf course design. I have always kept in the back of my mind, however, the guiding principle that an amateur golfer who shoots 110 needs to have places he or she can bail out. That way they enjoy playing golf.

The older golf courses built in the 1920s and 1930s were a bit shorter in total yardage, and usually you could roll the ball onto the green. The technology at that time necessary to construct a golf course centered around horses and plows. The horses and the plows moved the earth and did all of the work.

Today, big bulldozers, scrapers, and heavy earth-moving equipment allow a greater quantity of earth to be moved in a much shorter amount of time. However, the price that the golf course itself pays is that the natural landscape has been adversely affected. The effect of this natural landscape being upset is important. The effect on the golf ball itself is tremendous. The older courses were very natural and playable and could easily be maintained. They were, and still are, a nice walk through nature. They are, however, few and far between, as they have yielded to more modern courses.

How I actually put pen to paper and officially started designing golf courses was quite by accident. I was riding on an airplane and was sitting next to Brent Wadsworth of Wadsworth Construction, the premier golf course construction company. We talked for a while about golf and golf course design. After hours of talking, one thing led to another and he put me in touch with Roger Packard, the golf course designer. Roger and I ended up working together for ten years designing golf courses and having a lot of fun in the process. A neat aspect of golf course design is that it gives me a break from playing golf and is enjoyable for me.

The natural landscape of the designated area should dictate at all times how the golf course is going to be designed. I always enjoy working a golf course through the landscape, as opposed to bulldozing in a lake where it doesn't fit from an aesthetic point of view. The best golf course is the one that is created and within five years someone will come out and play a hole and ask if the course has been there for forty years. You'd like it all to fit in well with the landscape. I've seen golf courses where all of a sudden there is a green stuck out in the middle of nowhere and it makes no sense. To me, the placement of the greens and the bunkers all need to make sense with the natural flowing landscapes.

The easiest aspect of designing a golf course is to make a particular hole hard. The harder aspect of golf course design is to make a hole playable for the thirty-handicapper and harder for the better player. If you can do this, you've really achieved something.

However, designing a golf course is often rewarding and heartbreaking at the same time. You can't make a hill a foot shorter, or move a green, if it's not properly placed. Everyone's money has been spent to create this mecca and sometimes it falls a bit short of perfection.

However, if a player can accept the ups and downs of designing a golf course, then they should go into golf course design because the rewards last a lifetime.

34. The U.S. Open

One of my favorite tournaments on tour is the U.S. Open.

The U.S. Open, unlike the Masters, is not played at the same course every year. The course varies from year to year. It could be held at Cherry Hills one year, then at Pinehurst another year. The USGA is in charge of the U.S. Open and they designate a course years before the tournament will be played there. What always intrigues me about the Open is that when the USGA takes over a club, the club becomes radically different in many respects. They have many modifications made to that course to the point where it's harder than any course you'll ever play in your life.

The rough is five inches long, as opposed to the usual one and a half inches. The rough is not only long off the fairway, but it's long around the greens as well. This is to make sure that any errant shot will cost a player. If a player misses the green, the odds are tremendous that he or she will not be able to get the ball onto the green in the next shot. If a player drives the ball into the rough off the tee, the player will often have to take out their sand wedge and chop it back onto the fairway just to lift the ball out of that terribly deep rough. The third shot will be the one that should have been the second shot. Usually, the players will be penalized anywhere from one-third of a shot to one-half of a shot on any given hole if they are errant and hit the ball into the rough. This adds up, and if you drive the ball in the rough on two different holes the probability is that you will make only one par. *Ouch!*

Even if the lie in the rough is playable, the player will probably have to drive it out of the rough with so much force that there won't be enough spin on the ball to save the ball from rolling off the intensely fast greens. So, if the rough doesn't hurt you, the faster-than-the-speed-of-light greens will finish you for that hole. It is absolutely essential to hit every fairway and put enough spin on the ball so as to stabilize it on the green.

The USGA also makes sure that for the U.S. Open the fairways are narrowed and the greens are faster and firmer. All factors combined, the golf course is about eight shots harder than it usually is for that particular golf course. They want to identify the best player for that week. I feel that the USGA sets up the U.S. Open to be the most difficult tournament. The U.S. Open is not just about playing golf, it's about survival.

Players not only have to survive the conditions but they also have to fight against their own emotions. That makes this tournament the hardest of the majors in my book. Sometimes making a bogey is not bad in a U.S. Open. The key is not to make double-bogey or triple-bogey. The USGA takes a par-72 golf course and makes the par 5's par 4's, and the course becomes a par-70 one. This greatly affects the golfer's psyche. Whereas a golfer felt like he was in his comfort zone, now he feels uneasy. This is especially true if the pro golfer has played the course before many times. Now the par-5 holes on which he was accustomed to making birdie or eagle become par-4 holes, and a struggle ensues to make par on those holes.

The U.S. Opens often have hard, fast greens and deep rough around the greens whereby if you misplayed your shot, you were in trouble. It is in that instance where the tour player will tell himself to play for the bunker. If you're a good bunker player, you can get the ball up and in out of the bunker. If you know that you can play the bunker well, then you won't be worried about making an aggressive shot with the ball possibly landing in the bunker.

The sadder reality is that Cherry Hills, where I won and where Arnold Palmer had his famous win, will not see many more U.S. Opens played there because the USGA must answer to the corporations who sponsor the U.S. Open, and they want hospitality tents and more amenities rather than the historic aspect. Pinehurst had many courses so it could house a U.S. Open, where Payne Stewart won in 1999. Bethpage, the Black Course, site of the 2002 U.S. Open, has the room for the corporations, and that is a beautiful course and it will go down in history as one of the great golf courses of all time.

Courses such as Marion in Philadelphia, Pennsylvania, and Inverness, in Toledo, Ohio, are two other beautiful golf courses that won't be seeing many more U.S. Opens because they are one-course golf courses. They just can't house the corporate hospitality tents and don't have the land for parking and corporate parties. Golf has become such a corporate event and such a big media–covered sport that space is crucial. Much to my chagrin, these two beautiful courses won't be hosting many more U.S. Opens and it's a huge blow to the game of golf that this has happened because both courses are legendary. Oakland Hills and Winged Foot have other golf courses, so the U.S. Open will still be played there.

Shorter courses, and courses that demand shot making and imagination, are the cornerstone of U.S. Open golf. Even today the USGA has its job cut out for it in taking courses without great history behind them and making them U.S. Open caliber.

35. The ProAm

◀

First and foremost, playing in a ProAm is one of the most enjoyable experiences in all of golf. It's a chance to mingle with some of the greatest of people anywhere. I've played golf with presidents, senators, House speakers, congressmen, businessmen, and entertainers.

I've played at ProAms where corporate executives have come over to me and asked me for advice. I've played with guys who have given me these odd looks and have then proceeded to tell me that this was their first time ever on a golf course. This happens more than you might think. To this person, I always give the following speech:

"Golf is not the easiest game in the world, and you won't pick it up in five minutes. So, the focus for this day is to enjoy the surroundings and the company of the other people in your group and at the event. If you screw up, it's no big deal. Have fun. If you whiff it and hit it ten feet, we don't care. Just try to do your best and just enjoy being out here."

In addition to this pep talk, I will give them some pointers on their grip, their stance, their ball placement, and their club selection. Most of all, however, I'll tell them "don't worry about hitting the ball, just swing the club." Oh yes, and have fun! If you can't have fun at a ProAm, there is something wrong with you. The whole day is one of golf, eating, talking, and laughing. What's not fun about those things?

However, if they are really concerned with the game of golf from a mechanical standpoint because they are a good player and they want to improve, I'll always try and help them.

The biggest problem of golf swings at ProAms is that too many people try to hit the ball, instead of just swinging the golf club. Maybe it's because they're nervous or because they want to be able to hit the ball a long way their first time up and show everyone they can do it. Whatever the reason, the most important lesson is to make club-face contact with the ball by just naturally swinging the club.

It's amazing that sometimes these pure beginners go out, hit some good shots, and end up liking golf! To me, that's the ultimate compliment, and it's a great feeling. To think that by being there I might have made someone enthusiastic about the game of golf is incredible. In fact, I've seen some familiar faces over the years at those same corporate outings, and I'll reminisce with them about that first on-course lesson. I'll kid them about that first day and how they've since become avid golfers and have officially caught the "sickness" of the game of golf. It's a neat feeling for me when they exhibit that love of the game!

My most memorable ProAm was played in 1977 at the Westchester Country Club. I got paired with Tip O'Neill, Dan Rostenkowski, Jamie Whitten, and Howard Evans. They were guests of Stewart Klein, and they thought their pro was going to be Dave Stockton. A tournament glitch happened, and they got me. At the onset no one was very happy about it. But that all changed. The day was thankfully shortened by rain. I was playing awful, so we sat inside and talked and ate. I went on to win the tournament that week, and they all took credit for helping me correct my swing! I received a photo/press album from Tip O'Neill and congratulations from the rest. Danny was instrumental in me and my family meeting President Reagan in the Oval Office, for which I am very thankful. The best thing that came out of the day, though, is my friendship with Stewart Klein. He and his family hold a special place in my life.

You name it, and it's happened in ProAms. I've seen people make a shot in which their golf ball will hit a tree, then ricochet back and hit them. I saw one guy break his ankle by hitting himself there with a ball. It was on his second shot. He hit that shot so far on the heel of the club that the ball bounced and creamed him in the ankle and broke it. In a ProAm in 2001 at the Ford Senior, an amateur lined up his putt on the seventeenth green and he backed off and fell into the lake! ProAms are seldom boring!

36. My Broadcasting Career and Friends at ESPN

My whole life changed when I began broadcasting because I now had another dimension to my career in professional golf. It all started when Andy Young and Steve Beim, the producer and director of golf on ESPN, called me in the early 1990s and asked me to work a Senior PGA event in Las Vegas. At that time my schedule was free and I was more than eager to accept their proposition. After that event they asked me, for two years in a row, to work more ESPN golf matches at the season's end. At that time I wanted to continue to play. I had made a decision at the time to place my broadcasting career on hold with regard to regularly broadcasting games. Gary Koch, who was involved with ESPN, broke his ankle at the Canadian Open one year and they asked me to replace him the next week in a tournament in which I was playing. I asked how it would work for me and they said if I didn't make the cut, I could do television on Friday and the rest of the week-end. I ended up working on Friday after my round. I worked the weekend for ESPN and enjoyed it.

ESPN asked me to work for them regularly. Bob Murphy was turning fifty and had decided to play on the SENIOR PGA TOUR. This would be a major step in my life, as it would signal my leaving playing on the PGA TOUR for the most part.

Susan and I sat down and decided it was time for me to accept this position with ESPN. At the time I wasn't playing well and I wasn't having any fun. This offer came at the end of the stretch where it seemed as if I was having an operation every single year. I decided television would be a great venue for me.

The crew that we worked with at the beginning was tremendous, and each new crew over the years has been terrific. We had an awful lot of fun, from the producers and directors to the cameramen. It became one big family, and we enjoyed being around each other. My analyst partners changed, and Jim Kelly was the original host. Bob Murphy was in the booth when I first started, and Gary Koch and I were out on the grounds together. After Bob left, Gary Koch moved into the booth, then Frank Beard was hired. Billy Kratzert was hired. Then Gary Koch left to go to NBC. Robert Wrenn came aboard. I worked on the ground and in the booth. Both venues are interesting to me because of the variety of qualities you can bring to television. The greatest thing about ESPN was that everyone got along really well and we all parked our egos and tried to give the fans a great golf show. What mattered was not who got credit for ideas, but that we were bringing new angles to golf to the fans.

What I tried to do as an announcer, and what I still try to accomplish in the broadcast booth to this day, is to give the fans a new angle and new information. I always place myself in the position of the average fan. If I am a fan sitting at home, I want the announcer to tell me something that I don't know, not something that is common knowledge. It was very important to me to try and tell the viewers what the players were thinking about before they took their shot. I wanted the fans to know how the players were approaching each situation and why they were selecting the club they ended up selecting. Sometimes the layout of the hole dictated what club would be used, and I would tell this to the fans. I wouldn't just tell them that this player is hitting a six-iron and leave it at that, as that would be unfair to the fans. It's easy after the fact to tell someone what has transpired over the course of a hole, but they have already seen it with their own eyes. They saw the player four-putt or they saw the player hit a ball for eagle right into the bottom of the cup. They don't need me to overstate the obvious. I tried to tell the fans something interesting before it happened. I tried to tell them what the player was trying to accomplish and how he was going to accomplish it and what should happen on that particular shot.

On television things happen so quickly that you must make every conscious effort to be quick with your comments, or else the moment will pass. Oftentimes an athlete will go from being a full-time athlete to one who is also a part-time broadcaster. Sometimes when this happens the "player" part of the athlete is lost. I wanted to improve and I wanted to develop a style, but I did not want to sacrifice and lose that player spontaneity that I had when I first joined ESPN.

The one aspect of doing television is that there's no crash course in how to do it. You basically do the show on the fly and make mistakes and learn from those mistakes. You look at old tapes and you try to improve yourself in all ways possible. You just hope that you don't get fired by the time you've learned from your mistakes. The best method I used for self-improvement in the booth was trial and error.

The producers and directors were always offering me tips on how to improve. Some I listened to, some I didn't. I really owe a lot to Andy and Steve. They were very knowledgeable about golf and tops in their field.

The very first tournament at which I worked full-time for ESPN was in Tucson, Arizona. I was out with a group at Tucson National and unfortunately the course does not lend itself for broadcaster viewing. There aren't many places where you can get a great view if you're a roving announcer or a hole announcer. Also, the way it was set up, one's voice traveled well, and so I personally had to stand way back from the action because the last thing in the world I wanted was for the players to hear me and to get annoyed with me. Well, I thought I was being ingenious and so I climbed up on a camera tower. All of a sudden my director got excited with me. I hadn't realized what I had done, but what I had done was to move the camera and affect everyone's TV reception at ESPN and in viewers' homes. The picture being transmitted was a jumpy one. Even though my view was clear and my commentary was good, it didn't matter because everyone's screen was jumping up and down. I had messed up the picture with my tiny bit of movement. He very calmly told me that I was never to climb another camera tower ever again. He said, "Is that you out up there?" He knew from the movement inside his viewfinder that I was up on that tower. This was a good learning experience for me. It just goes to show you that you can think you're being smart by climbing a tower and you can wreak havoc in the process.

That same tournament I learned my second great lesson in golf broadcasting. I was interviewing the winner of the tournament during the trophy presentation and I allowed him to take control of the microphone. All of a sudden I hear in my ear, "Did you let go of the microphone? Get it back! You never, ever, let anybody take control of the microphone because then you lose all control." This was what the director had spoken in my ear, which is another interesting part of broadcasting (i.e., the things that the public doesn't hear but that we do, in our headsets and earpieces). The point wasn't whether the player would say anything inappropriate. The whole point was that if I gave up control of that microphone and ESPN had planned to cut to another scene, there would be a problem switching. I had now learned lesson number two: never give up the microphone to anyone.

One memorable broadcast Jim Kelly and I were in the booth at Charlotte, and the booth was hit by lightning. A tornado had ripped through the area and the roof was blown right off and lights came crashing down on us. It was scary. No one got hurt, but there were these live wires all over the place. We actually went off the air for a while. I couldn't believe that I was surrounded by all of these wires and I didn't get hurt. What happened was that the crew shut off the electricity and I managed to free myself.

The most difficult part to broadcasting is not answering the things said to you in your ear aloud on national television. Oftentimes, our producers will ask us questions at ESPN in our ears and will voice comments to us. If we were to answer them on the air, the whole world would be thinking to themselves, "What did he just say?" Every one of us has done that on television. I could be telling everyone that a specific player used a six-iron on a specific hole for a specific shot when he should have used a seven-iron, and meanwhile I'm hearing my director and producer speak to each other in my ear: You have to keep going and not stop speaking to the public. The producer and director will be informing us that "we're cutting to this scene or that scene" and the hardest part is paying attention to it.

The aspect of broadcasting that will keep me in the booth forever is that I'm speaking about something about which I care deeply—golf. John Madden is such a great football announcer because he cares about the NFL. He lives and breathes football and it reflects every time he takes to the broadcast booth. The passion for the game is what keeps us all going. After all, I've played this game called golf my whole life, and to speak about various aspects of it on national television is a great thrill. I've also had a lot of fun being around these great young players that we've seen in recent years.

"Sportscenter" was an added bonus that followed my initial tour of duty in the booth with ESPN. The heads at the station asked me to join the "Sportscenter" crew for the majors, and I have loved every minute of it.

To be at the majors that Tiger Woods has won has been a lot of fun for me. Just to be present there and on the scene to see Tiger win is a thrill. I've also had a lot of fun seeing Jack Nicklaus play in his last U.S. Open. The ESPN crew has become one big family. Chris

Berman and I have a great friendship. Mike Tirico and I are good friends, and I enjoy each time I get to work with Mike.

One of the more personal aspects of broadcasting has been covering stories and how to spin them. You can spin a story any way you want, but you must always bear the consequences. The consequences can be small or they can be great. The decision lies within the soul of the reporter. I know what it's like to be on the other end of a story that was spun in a disparaging way regarding my abilities as an athlete and with respect to playing hurt. I have consciously made an effort never to do that to someone else. I have tried never to spin stories the wrong way. It's not just a matter of opinion. If a player hits a poor shot, there are a lot of ways to communicate to the audience that the previous shot was a poor one. You can say that "he's a choker and can't play at all," or you can say, "He tried to play the shot *this* way and he couldn't pull it off." I prefer the latter because it doesn't attack the integrity of the athlete.

The one aspect of golf that I bring to the broadcast booth is that I do know the feeling of walking up the eighteenth fairway on Sunday ready to be crowned a champion at a major. There aren't a lot of guys broadcasting who can tell you what it feels like to be a champion. They can tell you what they think it must feel like to win, but they can't tell you how it actually feels to take that trophy home. I have had the experience of waking up the next morning only to rub my eyes and realize that it wasn't a dream, that I actually won the U.S. Open, and I'm proud to be one of the select few that has had that wonderful experience happen to me twice in my life. My golfing career and my announcing career have meshed well.

There have been Kelly, Koch, Murphy, and the rest of the guys with whom I started out in television. These were the guys from whom I learned. Frank Beard and Robert Wrenn were great to be around, and they came along right after Murphy. When I got involved with

"Sportscenter," new people entered my life: Karl Ravech, Chris Berman, and Mike Tirico. Mike can do everything and anything. He is as good as anybody there is in all of television in my opinion. Karl is a fantastic and fun guy to be around. He makes those "Sportscenter" satellite desk moments a lot of fun.

Chris Berman is an experience in himself. Chris is Chris. When you work alongside Berman you realize that you're having as much fun in your life as you've ever had and you're loving every minute of it. You have no clue at all as to what might happen next! He keeps you on your toes at all times. Chris Berman is the Godfather of ESPN. He is Mr. ESPN. Jim Kelly, doing the Americas Cup, and Chris both deserve credit for putting ESPN on the map. Chris is a super superstar! He's a riot to work with, and working with him, it's as if we're two twelve-year-olds going off to work. I have a great time. Chris is so great with people that I love to compare him with Arnold Palmer. Although he has a tremendous worldwide following, Chris Berman will take the time to make every fan of ESPN that comes over feel special. He talks, he signs autographs, and he tells stories.

We were at the U.S. Open in Oakland Hills, and Gary Koch and I were doing the show with him. One night during our show, we were to air live at midnight; it was slightly afterward and we were attacked by these hummingbird-sized bugs. The entire show was done without knowing what was coming next, and to make the night even crazier, halfway through our live program the front of the ESPN logo on our desk fell off! It was one of those nights that was absolutely crazy. Welcome to live television!

In 1999 Chris, myself, Tirico, and Karl Ravech were doing the U.S. Open special at Pinehurst. The show was supposed to come on the air live at 12:30 A.M. This was also the special night the NHL Stanley Cup Finals were on, and the game went into three overtimes! So, for three overtimes, there we sat in the booth on the vacant, dark, desolate

U.S. Open grounds. We had been there for fifteen hours. Every time the game went into another overtime, it meant one more hour delay for us. We ended up doing the show at 3:00 A.M., and by the time we came on, heavy rains came down into our set. We ended up getting soaked and holding these huge umbrellas over ourselves to try to keep dry. The ability to think on your feet and improvise is a must when doing live television.

The neat thing about having done all of this golf for television was that it kept me close to the game even while I wasn't playing. ESPN also afforded me the opportunity to get to some golfers and to know the real men behind some often misunderstood people. Two such men are Craig Stadler and Jim Colbert. Craig Stadler is portrayed as a grouchy type of person, but he is one of the greatest guys in the world to play alongside, and he's a ball of laughs off the course. He is always gregarious, and you can approach him and speak with him about almost anything.

Jim Colbert is perceived as cocky and arrogant. Even some players perceive him to be that way. This could not be further from the truth. Here is a guy who would do anything in the world for you, and he's helped more people than a lot of us golfers put together. Jim is so generous with his time and money for charity that he knows no limits. I got to know Jim well when I was covering golf for ESPN, and I saw this man treat an entire crew of workers, lighting workers and cameramen, to a round of golf. Jim would host "events," consisting of golf, an elaborate dinner, and prizes for the workers behind the scenes at ESPN. All at his expense, not on the corporate books. He loved every minute of it. Once he was on the SENIOR PGA TOUR, he loved treating people to rounds of golf, organizing charity dinners. After battling prostate cancer, Jim goes around and plays in golf classics to benefit prostate cancer all at his own expense. If I needed help, he'd be one of the first guys I would call, because he is so caring and understanding. I have ESPN to thank for my continued friendship with Jim. We won the Mutual Legends of Golf tournament together in 2000 and 2001.

37. The SENIOR PGA TOUR: These Guys Are Good

I knew what I was getting involved with even before I turned fifty in March 2000. The quality of play I was witnessing amazed me, week in and week out. I was pleasantly surprised that many players at fifty are better than they were earlier in their career. Maybe that's because when these guys started out playing in the early 1970s every dollar mattered, and they needed the money to raise their family. The pressure was enormous, and it affected their quality of play. I'm not sure why many players play better now than at thirty, but maybe it's because the pressure is off them now to win for the sake of needing money, and they are at a different stage of maturity in their lives.

The SENIOR PGA TOUR is a great opportunity for me to play golf again in a competitive manner against some of the same players I grew up playing years ago. I did not play well my first year on the Senior Tour, even though I started off by winning the Mutual Legends of Golf Classic with Jim Colbert. For me, to be able to do what I love—play golf—twice in my life at different stages is great. Is the Senior Tour a perfect system? No, it's not. The Senior Tour is a combination of quality play and competition, but also nostalgia. The Senior Tour was so strong in the late 1980s and early 1990s that it was giving the regular tour a problem. Arnold was playing quite a bit, and

Chi Chi and Lee Trevino were at their best. Ray Floyd was playing quite a bit. In 1995 things changed again when Tiger Woods came upon the PGA TOUR. The SENIOR PGA TOUR now lost some fans because Arnold and Chi Chi were getting older, and these marquee names have cut back on their playing time. We need to do a better job in creating a better product, both in quality play and in entertaining fans. Some of the players don't understand that at all. It's really important to have good fan relations.

Cadillac is a great sponsor and is perfect for us. The demographics are right for us, as the company caters to older people with money. Charles Schwab is a great sponsor because everyone is looking for investment strategies. For corporate sponsors, one nice aspect of golf is that a company can really target distinct communities. Hale Irwin and Bruce Fleisher have accomplished quite a lot and have tirelessly promoted the Senior tour. Bruce won the National Amateur and then was touted as the great new player and struggled on tour. He quit the tour and became a club professional. He consequently learned a lot more about his golf swing and himself through working as a club pro, and when he returned in his forties he played well on the PGA TOUR. Once he turned fifty and entered the Senior Tour, he played exceptionally well.

The SENIOR PGA TOUR courses have been designed so that the conditions reward great driving and great putting. The rough is not quite as long on the Senior Tour. The green speeds aren't quite as fast, but they're getting there. We're playing golf courses that are not seven or eight hundred yards shorter than the PGA TOUR courses, as they were at one time, but only two hundred yards shorter.

Most people our age are thinking of retirement, but we're out there playing hard. It's the ultimate mulligan, for me, to be able to play golf competitively all over again in my early fifties.

38. Thank You, Golf

I feel as if I have played golf in the greatest era. Arnold, Jack, Lee, and Gary were still very competitive. Sam Snead was nearing the end of his illustrious career, but he was out there, and it was fun to be beside him. Tom Watson, Tom Kite, and Hale Irwin were just beginning on the road to success. I got the chance to play with these men and see them win in front of me. This generation, because they didn't make a ton of money, took every shot seriously. The late 1960s saw George Archer miss the top-60 money list by $1.50. Think about it! There must have been a time when he backhanded a shot or made some minor mistake, and that cost him being an exempt player. It's pretty serious business when one dollar and fifty cents separates you from the top. Today the players take more chances and play more aggressively because the money is there for them to grab. Making the cuts back in the 1960s and early 1970s was a big deal. If you made the cut, you played the next week, and for a non-exempt player that was critical. This isn't a worry for today's players.

I have so much enjoyed my golfing experiences with President Gerald R. Ford. President Ford is a gifted athlete and a very good golfer. He has a fourteen handicap. He caught a lot of grief about hitting these horrible shots. He was a great skier, and an outstanding college football player at the University of Michigan. He hit long and some-times a ball would be errant, as has happened to us all. He was living in Vail, Colorado, when I represented the Vail Beaver Creek Resort. We played quite a bit of golf together. He was a great golf talker. He loved talking golf on the golf course. He wanted tips on playing better.

President Reagan loved the game of golf. Susan, my daughters, and I were at the White House, and President Reagan personally told me that golf was so important to him when he was in Hollywood that he would play whenever he wasn't making movies. He wouldn't just play occasionally, he'd play every single day. He said he would make a movie and it would take up all of his time and then when the shooting of the movie was complete he would have about four months off between that film and his next film. He would go out and play golf every day. He said that at the beginning his handicap wasn't that great, but as the days went along he got on a hot streak. At the beginning the actors were sending cabs for him because they couldn't wait for him to play with them, so they could take all his money. By the time a month was out, he was sending cabs for them taking their money! Each time he had a long layoff he would be a bit rusty at the begin-ning and then after a month he was back to his true form as an excel-lent golfer.

Dan Quayle and I first became associated when he was a congress-man in Indiana. He was a scratch player! He was terrific on the golf course and, although his handicap wasn't as good after he became vice president, he was still a single-digit handicapper. Dan still had that schoolchild love of golf even after he became vice president.

Tip O'Neill and Dan Rostenkowski and I played a lot of golf when Tip was the Speaker of the House and Dan was the chairman of the Ways and Means Committee. We played a lot of golf together and Dan was a good golfer. Tip was the ultimate sports fan, and he loved golf. His game was not as good as it could have been, but he loved to play in ProAms. They loved intermixing with people and politicking.

Politicians are always running for office—even on the golf course! They talk. They hit the ball. They talk some more, whether it's golf or social events, they're out having a great time of it. The best part about playing with politicians was that they had an ability to make you feel comfortable in every way. They made you feel like a star, but everyone knew they were the real stars. The stories they told were impressive. After eighteen holes and a nice lunch or dinner, you would be full of stories to retell at your own parties.

Even my daughters were afforded the opportunity to meet presidents and senators and important people. Andrea was a little girl when I won the U.S. Open in the 1980s and we were all set to go to Washington, D.C., to meet President Reagan. She was nervous and was actually distressed about meeting the president. We told her she'd be fine and she could do it. She had wanted one of those Cabbage Patch dolls, and we told her if she could meet the president, extend her hand, and speak with him as an adult, we'd buy her one. She agreed—with an extra ten bucks thrown in—the ultimate agent. We went to Washington, met the president, and she walked right up to Ronald Reagan and extended her hand and spoke with him and it was great. When he complimented her she jumped up and said, "I did it!" We have a picture of her all excited and Reagan laughing as hard as ever.

Golf has been so great to me. It has enabled me to win in front of millions on television, have my photo on the cover of *Sports Illustrated*, appear on national television, and begin a new career as a broadcaster. Golf is the greatest, and the people who play this sport are genuine athletes with true abilities. They play hard, they play hurt, and they are the best.

I hope that all of you who have read this book feel better about your own golf game and about yourselves. Golf is all about feeling good. Golf is something that everyone can do from age three onward for the rest of their lives.

To me, the game of golf mirrors life. There are the bogeys, the

Tom Watson, me, and Bob Murphy at Bob's fiftieth birthday party

putts, and birdies. Every now and then you get a double-bogey or an eagle, on the happier side. Golf can be thought provoking, funny, and dramatic—just like life. I have enjoyed my golf career on the PGA tour, my continuing career as a broadcaster at ESPN with my friends Chris Berman, Mike Tirico, and Karl Ravech, and my new career as a player on the SENIOR PGA TOUR. I'm thankful for the corporate sponsors I've met through the SENIOR PGA TOUR.

I can only close this book by saying that golf should be a game associated with the idea of having fun. It is the sport that transcends time. You can play it as most any age. My wish is that all of you have long drives, great fairway shots, putts for an eagle, and the coveted hole-in-one, and may the wind be at your back and the sun shine brightly upon your golf ball. I hope that all of you out there have enjoyed this book, and most important, I hope that you pass on this knowledge and love of golf to a youngster so that the game of golf may live on forever.